The Complete Sleep Guide for Contented Babies and Toddlers

The Complete Sleep Guide for Contented Babies and Toddlers

Gina Ford

Vermilion
LONDON

For Contented Babies, their parents
and the generations to come

1 2 3 4 5 6 7 8 9 10

First published in the United Kingdom in 2003
by Vermilion, an imprint of Ebury Press
Random House UK Ltd
Random House
20 Vauxhall Bridge Road
London SW1V 2SA

Random House Australia (Pty) Limited
20 Alfred Street, Milsons Point, Sydney,
New South Wales 2061, Australia

Random House New Zealand Limited
18 Poland Road, Glenfield, Auckland 10, New Zealand

Random House (Pty) Limited
Endulini, 5A Jubilee Road, Parktown 2193, South Africa

Random House UK Limited Reg. No. 954009
www.randomhouse.co.uk

Papers used by Vermilion are natural recyclable products
made from wood grown in sustainable forests.

A CIP catalogue record for this book is available from the British Library

ISBN: 0 09 188755 0

Printed and bound in Great Britain by
Mackays of Chatham plc, Chatham, Kent

Contents

Acknowledgements

To all the parents who have shared their babies with me I would like to say a very special thank you. Your trust and faith in me and the constant support and feedback you have given me over the years has enabled me to learn so much about the sleeping habits of babies and young children, and make this book possible. In particular I would like to say a special thank you to Françoise and Steven Skelly; Helen and David Sherbourne; Juliette and Alistair Scott; and Julie and Alvin Stardust.

As always, my family and friends have been there for me throughout the writing of this book. Thank you Aunt Jean and Uncle Dan, and cousins Ann Clough and Sheila Eskdale for your love, support and encouragement, and for helping look after my darling Molly.

I would also like to thank my friends Jane Revell, Carla Fodden Flint and Sandra Gregory for their friendship, encouragement and support. My dear friend and fantastic personal trainer Robert Redpath deserves a big thank you for his patience and support in helping me come to terms with my procrastination regarding exercise and fear of computers!

Thank you to Fiona MacIntyre, Lesley McOwan, Julia Kellaway and all the team at Random House – you have all been fantastic in helping me get my message across to parents. A huge thank you to Becky Bagnell for your valuable input and comments and for doing a great job of making sense of my manuscripts.

Emma Todd, my wonderful agent, continues to give me enormous help, support and encouragement and manages to guide me with tremendous patience, great humour and sensitivity. Dear Emma, a very special thank you. I am eternally grateful to you for always being there for me and having such faith in me.

Darling Molly, despite going thought the terrible two's while writing this book you are still following the Contented Little Baby routines and continue to bring much love, laughter and happiness into my life – you deserve a very special and loving thank you.

Finally, thank you to all the readers who have taken the time to contact me. Your opinions and suggestions are very important to me, as are you warm wishes and support. Special love and thanks to you all and to your contented babies.

Foreword

There is much conflicting advice from childcare experts on how to tackle sleep problems and at what age a routine or sleep-training can be introduced. The majority of experts advise parents with very young babies who are waking up several times a night to wait until the baby is six months old before attempting sleep-training. My own personal view is that the longer parents put off trying to resolve excessive night-time waking, the harder it will be to solve problems further down the line.

Since the publication of my first book, *The Contented Little Baby Book*, in 1999, and then *Contented Baby to Confident Child*, I have been contacted by thousands of parents who share my belief as they struggle to cope with older babies and children who wake several times a night. The fact that a huge number of these parents have to register on a waiting list to get advice from one of the 126 sleep clinics in this country would also confirm that we have a serious problem with our children's excessive night-time waking.

I believe that prevention is better than cure and if parents were to take control and structure their babies' feeding and sleeping needs from very early on, a huge number of sleeping problems could be avoided.

Contrary to what my critics claim, my books are not about teaching babies to sleep through the night by denying feeds or leaving them to cry. My methods are about teaching parents to recognise their babies' different needs from a very early age, enabling them to meet their needs long before crying and sleepless nights set in. However, if a baby has got into a routine of excessive night-time waking and developed the wrong sleep associations then this book is also designed to guide those particular children into better sleeping habits.

The practical advice this book contains is based on my personal experience of helping over 300 parents care for their babies and advising thousands more on how best to solve the problem of excessive night-time waking. Sadly for babies and toddlers who are waking up several times because they have already developed wrong sleep associations, there is no simple cure. But if you are prepared to be consistent and persistent there are many solutions and case histories in this book that will help you establish a good sleeping pattern. Once you have established a good sleeping pattern the step-by-step guides on what to expect and what to aim for will help keep your baby on track.

1

Understanding Sleep

While the amount of sleep that individual babies need does vary and constantly changes as they grow, having a better understanding of sleep means you will be much more able to determine whether your baby or toddler has, or is possibly developing, a long-term sleep problem. Before attempting any form of routine or sleep-training it is imperative that you have a basic understanding of the different stages of sleep that babies and young children experience. Like adults, babies and children drift in and out of different stages of sleep. Parents who do not fully understand these different stages of sleep often disturb what is a natural progression of the different sleep cycles. When the baby stirs during a light stage of sleep, he will, if allowed and not needing a feed, usually return to a deeper stage of sleep. Parents who assume that these stirrings are caused by hunger and rush to the baby too quickly to try and get him back to sleep, often create long-term sleep association problems without realising. Once the wrong sleep associations are created it will be very difficult for a baby to sleep a longer stretch. A baby who is always rocked, fed or given a dummy to get to sleep will be much more likely to continue to wake several times a night, long after the age when he needs a feed to get him through the night. Because he will naturally come into a light sleep several times a night, he will more than likely need the same comfort to get him back to sleep. This can lead to excessive night-time wakings, sometimes until a child is nearly three years of age.

Sleep cycles

Sleep is divided into two cycles called REM (Rapid Eye Movement) sleep, usually referred to as light sleep, and non-REM sleep, usually referred to as deep sleep. A newborn baby goes straight into REM sleep when he first goes to sleep. During this light sleep his breathing becomes irregular, his body may twitch or jerk, his eyelids will flicker and his eyes appear to roll. He may even smile or frown during this cycle of light sleep. This sleep is often described as active sleep because a baby uses more oxygen and energy than during non-REM sleep. A baby who has gone full term will spend 50 per cent of his sleep cycle in REM sleep. A premature baby will spend 80 per cent in REM. The rest of the sleep cycle is spent in non-REM sleep.

During non-REM sleep the baby's breathing will be slow and regular. There are no eye movements and only the occasional twitch or jerk of the body. This calm sleep cycle is often described as quiet sleep. It allows the baby's mind and body to recharge, enabling him to cope with his next awake period. Research also shows us that this deep sleep is essential for the healthy development of a baby's mental and physical growth.

Dr Richard Ferber says that non-REM sleep is well developed at birth but has not evolved the four distinct stages experienced by older children and adults. It is not until the second month that a sequence of non-REM sleep stages begins to develop. When a baby of three months is ready to sleep, he first enters Stage One of non-REM – a drowsy sleep – then quickly passes into Stage Two – a light sleep – before reaching Stages Three and Four – very deep sleep. This whole non-REM cycle lasts around 40–50 minutes. The baby then passes to the REM sleep cycle (light sleep), which usually lasts 5–10 minutes, before returning to another cycle of non-REM sleep.

I have observed that it is between the ages of eight and twelve weeks that many parents begin to experience problems with their baby's day-time sleep, as the different stages of non-REM sleep begin to develop. During the first few weeks the majority of babies will tend to fall asleep easily – often in their car seat or in their pram in the corner of the sitting room – and frequently sleeping for several hours at a time. Unfortunately, as the baby's sleep cycle develops into more distinct stages of light and deep sleep, he will often find it more difficult to settle back to sleep after the 40–50 minute sleep cycle if he is used to sleeping in a day-time atmosphere. Although his body clock may need more sleep, particularly in the middle of the day, he will often find it difficult to get himself back to sleep. As the day progresses, the baby gets more and more irritable, and by late afternoon he is often very over-tired and fights sleep even more. Parents who don't realise that this fractious behaviour is caused by too short a nap in the middle of the day resort to feeding, rocking, patting, etc. to help him get back to sleep when he has come into his light sleep.

What starts out as a day-time sleep problem soon also becomes a night-time sleep problem. The baby who needs assistance to return to sleep when he comes into a light sleep during the day will more likely than not come to need the same help at night. Because all babies will come into a light sleep several times a night once they have developed an adult sequence of sleep cycles, a problem can soon evolve. This can often mean several wakings a night for parents for many months and sometimes years.

Where to sleep

I believe it is very important that from the early days a baby gets used to having his own space for sleep-times. Whether it is in a separate nursery or a corner in your bedroom, it is important, particularly in the very early days, to establish sleep-times in the cot away from the hustle and bustle of everyday activities. Establishing a sleeping area for your baby or toddler away from the rest of the house is not being cruel or selfish. It teaches him to relax and be happy in his own company, and to sleep without the assistance of adults.

Ensuring that your baby or toddler is comfortable is also essential when establishing good sleep habits, as it eliminates the possibility of night wakings due to discomfort. Getting the room temperature right so that he is neither too hot nor too cold is very important, as is dressing him in comfortable clothing for sleeping.

The following guidelines list the main causes of discomfort for babies and toddlers.

Room temperature

The ideal room temperature should be 18°C (64°F). Allowing a young baby to sleep in an overheated room not only contributes to the risk of cot death but also dries the mucous membranes of the nose. This can cause great discomfort to the baby and some medical experts claim it makes them more vulnerable to colds and infection. A battery-operated room thermometer is the best way to ensure that your baby's room is kept at the correct temperature. Some models are designed with an alarm that will sound if the temperature goes below or above the ideal level.

The cot or bed should not be positioned near a radiator, window or outside wall. The bedding for the cot when the baby is very young should be 100 per cent cotton. Quilts, bumpers and pillows should be avoided as they can cause overheating, which will not only cause your baby to be very unsettled but is also considered to be a major factor in cot death. During the first month if you are swaddling your baby it is also very important to reduce the layers of bedding on the cot or Moses basket, so that you avoid overheating. I would advise putting older babies, who are moving around the cot, and toddlers in a sleeping bag, as this avoids the problem of them getting cold if they get out from under the covers. I would delay transferring a toddler to a bed until about three years of age, at which time they will not need a sleeping bag as they are usually capable of covering themselves up.

In very hot weather it is advisable during the day to pull down the black-out blind halfway to avoid the room becoming overheated by early evening. Babies and toddlers can become very irritable in hot weather and may benefit from a fan in the room. Ensure that it does not blow directly on the baby and that it can not be reached by a child who is sleeping in a bed.

It is also important to remember to reduce the layers of bedding in hot weather. On particularly hot nights a nappy, vest and very thin sheet to half swaddle a tiny baby is all that is needed, with a thin sheet across the top. After the 10/11pm feed the baby can be put into his normal night clothes if the temperature has dropped, and after the 2/3am feed an additional thin cotton blanket may be added.

In hot weather it is essential that you keep a very close check that your baby does not become overheated, as this can not only cause great discomfort to the baby but is potentially dangerous.

With older babies and toddlers a nappy and T-shirt is usually enough during the early part of the night. They may need a very light-weight sleeping bag or to be covered with a thin blanket or sheet at your bedtime.

The best way to check if your baby is too hot or too cold is to feel the back of his neck. The layers of bedding and baby's clothing should them be adjusted accordingly.

Swaddling

For several weeks after birth many babies will twitch and startle when they drift in and out of sleep, sometimes so much that they wake themselves up. Some babies will go through this twitching stage when drifting off to sleep. This reaction is called the Moro reflex and is often very strong in the early days. These sudden jerky movements can be very upsetting to a baby as he does not realise that the sensations he is feeling are being caused by his own body movements. I believe that nearly all babies benefit from being swaddled in the first few weeks, provided it is done properly.

The following guidelines should help ensure that your baby is swaddled correctly, which will help him feel more secure and – provided he is well fed – help him sleep more soundly until his next feed is due.

The choice of swaddling blanket is important. Traditionally, babies were swaddled in hand-knitted shawls. These were ideal because they were usually very soft, fine and stretchy, which meant that the baby could be wrapped securely but still be allowed some movement and, more importantly, did not become overheated. Unfortunately, it is very difficult to obtain these shawls nowadays and many parents resort to using small cellular blankets, which in my opinion are never large enough to wrap the baby securely, and because of the thickness could possibly cause overheating. When I worked as a maternity nurse I used to make my own swaddling blankets. They were very basic, but they did the trick of keeping the baby secure without the risk of being too tight or overheating the baby.

To make two swaddling sheets all you need is 2m (2 yd) of stretch cotton T-shirt fabric, available from any department store or haberdashery shop. The fabric is usually 48 inches wide, which may seem enormous the first week or two, but does allow for growth. Cut the fabric into two lengths and make a hem of 2cm (1in) along the bottom and up both sides, then fold down a double hem of 4cm (2in) at the top. It is important that the hem that goes around the baby's neck is deep and secure.

Because the swaddling blanket is rectangular as opposed to square it allows extra fabric to go around the back of the baby, making the swaddle more secure. One of the reasons babies get out of a square swaddle is that once the first arm has been tucked in and the fabric tucked under the baby's back, there is not usually enough fabric to take right under the baby's back once the second arm has been tucked in.

I used to get my clients to practise on a large teddy. Once you have done it 20 or so times with a teddy, it becomes easier to get it right with the baby in the shortest time possible. One of the reasons that so many babies cry when they are being swaddled is because of the time it takes, not because they actually dislike being swaddled.

Another reason many babies get upset when they are being swaddled is that parents pull their arms down by their sides to wrap them. Most babies hate this, as they feel more secure with their arms across their chests. I always swaddled my babies kimono-style, which involves making little pockets within the swaddle so that the blanket is wrapped around their arms before being taken across the chest and the excess blanket tucked around the back.

The basic steps for contented baby swaddling are:

- Lay swaddling on a large flat surface such as your bed or the floor and position your baby so that he is more to the right side of the blanket than the left, but ensure that there is enough blanket to the right for it to be able to stretch across his body and around his back. You should also ensure that the top of the blanket is slightly higher than the back of his neck.

- Take the top corner of the right-hand side of the blanket and pull it up and away from your baby's neck.

- Take your baby's left hand in your right hand, pointing it outwards from his body, then with your left hand draw the right-hand side of the swaddle blanket across your baby's chest. Gently tug it downwards so that the 4cm (2in) border is sitting firmly around your baby's neck.

- The baby's left hand and your right hand will now be under the swaddle material. Place your free hand on top of your baby's chest, which is now covered by a layer of swaddle material. Then, using your right hand, bring your baby's left hand across his chest, so that it is as if you have made a sleeve. Tuck the excess blanket around his back and under his bottom (think kimono).

- Repeat the same procedure with your baby's right hand. Hold it up and outwards in your left hand, then with your right hand bring the remainder of the swaddling blanket across his chest. Take the arm wrapped in the blanket across his chest, tucking the excess under his back and bottom.

This swaddle ensures that your baby cannot wriggle free. He feels secure because he has his hands across his chest, but he can also move them around within the little pockets that you have created.

Once you have established regular feeding times and sleep-times you should start to get your baby used to being half swaddled. Start off by leaving the second arm out. Once he is happily sleeping with one arm out then you should progress to half swaddling him so that both his arms are out.

It is very important that you get your baby used to being half swaddled by the time he is two months old so that he is not at risk of overheating. It is also important at all times during the swaddling period to adjust the layers of clothing and bedding in accordance with the room temperature.

Bedding and clothing

Research shows us that throughout the night adults change position many times, adjusting pillows and bedding as they do so. Babies are not able to do this; therefore it is very important to ensure that your baby's bedding is not the cause of any discomfort. Care should be taken to ensure that mattress protectors, sheets and blankets are smooth and not crumpled. They also need to be tucked in securely so they cannot work their way loose or flap against the baby's face.

If you find that your baby or toddler is particularly wheezy or is coughing a lot when put in his cot, it is worthwhile paying particular attention to how you wash his bed linen. House mite droppings may be the cause, and ensuring that bed-linen is washed regularly at 15°C (60°F) is the only way to eliminate these, along with regular vacuuming of the mattress and carpets. It is also important to ensure that the window of the bedroom is left open for short spells to ensure that the room is adequately aired.

Try to make sure that the clothes you dress your baby or toddler in for bed are 100 per cent cotton. Polyester fabric does not allow the skin to breathe, and wool can bring some babies and young children out in a rash. When choosing vests, the best design is one called a bodysuit, which fastens under the legs. Avoid the

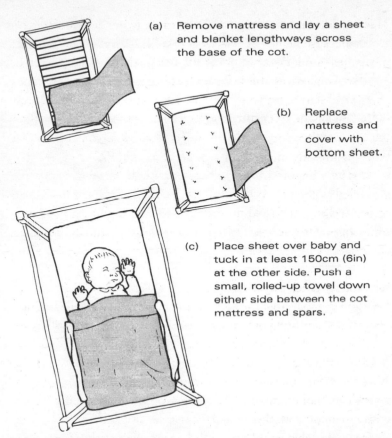

(a)   Remove mattress and lay a sheet and blanket lengthways across the base of the cot.

(b)   Replace mattress and cover with bottom sheet.

(c)   Place sheet over baby and tuck in at least 150cm (6in) at the other side. Push a small, rolled-up towel down either side between the cot mattress and spars.

traditional cross-over with ties, which can become undone and ride up, leaving the baby or toddler's chest bare and causing considerable discomfort. When choosing sleepsuits or nightdresses avoid styles with buttons at the back or large collars and fancy ribbons at the top or bottom that could flap across the baby's face or get caught around the baby's feet and cause irritation.

Pyjamas are also best avoided as the elastic waist on top of a bulky nappy can be very uncomfortable for a young baby or toddler.

When washing your baby's or toddler's clothes always check the inside. Remove any loose threads that could cause irritation and ensure that labels are ironed smooth or cut out.

Many trendy outfits are designed for style and not comfort;

therefore I suggest that for day-time sleeps your baby wears only his vest, and if it is cold an extra blanket can be added to the cot.

Toys, activity centres and overhead mobiles should all be removed when the baby or toddler is asleep in the cot. As a baby comes into a light sleep even a very soft toy can cause him to wake should he accidentally roll on to it. The sudden noise of an activity centre accidentally banged will certainly cause the majority of babies or toddlers to wake up crying with fright. In my experience, during the early days having toys of any description in the cot at sleeping times can be very confusing to babies. At this stage we are trying to establish the difference between feeding, sleeping and social time, and I believe that toys are best kept for the times when your baby is awake. During the second year many children will become attached to a certain toy and want to take it to bed. At this age I would allow one or two (preferably soft) toys in the cot, as the toddler is of an age when he has the sense to move the toy out of the way if he is uncomfortable.

Bed sharing

There is still a huge debate as to whether parents should take their babies into bed with them. Parents in favour of bed sharing claim that it is natural to have their babies with them at night and that co-sleeping actually helps establish breast feeding better than when the baby is settled in his own bed at night. Many experts also believe that parents who bed share with their baby actually have a closer bond with their baby than those who don't.

Some research also indicates that, provided parents follow certain safety precautions, bed sharing may actually help reduce the risk of cot death, because the closeness of the mother to her baby helps regulate his breathing. However, there is growing concern among many experts that parents who sleep with their baby may be putting them at greater risk. Statistics show that nearly 70 per cent of young babies who die in their first year were sleeping with parents at the time, either in the bed or on the sofa. Parents falling asleep on the sofa with a young baby is a major concern of The

Foundation for the Study of Infant Deaths, as it puts the baby at a great risk of sudden infant death syndrome (SIDS) or getting trapped and suffocating when over-tired parents accidentally fall asleep while feeding or cuddling their baby.

The current guidelines for safe bed sharing are as follows:

- Parents who smoke or have been drinking should not take their baby into bed, neither should parents who are over-weight or excessively tired.

- Parents who are on drugs or medication that cause drowsi-ness should also avoid taking their baby into bed.

- Parents should ensure that the baby is laid to sleep on his back, well away from the pillows. Sheets and blankets are preferable to duvets and quilts, which may cause the baby to overheat.

- The bed should be positioned so that the baby is not at risk of getting trapped between the mattress and the wall.

I have read of four deaths in the last year of very young babies who suffocated while sleeping with their parents. All of the parents had followed the above guidelines and none were overweight or smokers, or had been drinking or were overly tired. They simply took their baby to bed because they had read that it would create a better bond with their baby. All of these parents were devastated by the tragedy of losing a baby in such a way and heartbroken that they had not been informed that there is a risk of suffocation if par-ents choose to bed share with their baby. No matter how small it may be, it is important that you realise there is a risk of suffocation if you take your baby into bed with you, and you should think long and hard about whether you really want to put your baby at risk.

When I worked as a maternity nurse I always had the baby right next to my bed in a Moses basket and I would take him into bed to feed him but once he had been fed and started to get sleepy I would put him straight back into his basket. If he got very fussy I would bring him into bed again for a cuddle, but again when he got drowsy I would put him back into his basket. It was sometimes very tiring if I had a baby who took longer to settle, but at the end of the day I could never have lived with myself if anything had happened because I had fallen asleep with the baby.

My advice to parents who wish to have their baby close to them in the early days is to use a Moses basket or one of the specially designed cots that has a detachable side allowing it to be positioned right next to their bed, allowing them the closeness without putting the baby at risk.

Bed sharing and sleep associations

Bed sharing can also cause other problems in that a baby who becomes dependent on being cuddled to sleep in his parents' bed will find it more difficult at a later stage to settle himself to sleep in his own bed. In the early days it can be very exhausting trying to settle a fractious baby in his own bed. But in the long-term you also have to decide whether you have the energy to spend months and months of cuddling your baby to get him to sleep, and whether you are actually doing your baby more harm than good by teaching him to become dependent on you for getting to sleep. Every week I get dozens of calls from exhausted parents of older babies and toddlers who are taking hours to settle in the evening because they have become so dependent on their parents' presence to get to sleep. The whole family begins to suffer as sleep deprivation takes its toll, and most of the parents I speak to bitterly regret that they had not been made aware of the long-term problems of sleeping with their baby.

I believe it is a complete myth that parents who share their bed with their baby are more bonded with their babies than those who don't. In my experience bed sharing may make some parents feel closer to their babies, but more often than not it ends up with parents sleeping in separate rooms from each other and mothers becoming physically and mentally drained when night feeds go on long after the baby is big enough to sleep through without a feed. This situation puts enormous pressure on the family as a whole and the pleasure of family life soon disappears when over-tired parents try to cope with a fractious, demanding and over-tired baby during the day.

Sudden Infant Death Syndrome

Although it is still unclear what actually causes sudden infant death syndrome, or cot death as it is also called, studies in recent years have proved that putting babies to sleep on their backs during the first six months of life definitely reduces the risks. For the parents of some young babies with a very strong Moro reflex this can present a problem, as these babies can get very distressed when put down to sleep on their back. However, I know from experience that by perservering with these young babies the problem can be overcome. Ensuring that the baby is tucked in firmly so that he is unable to kick off his cover will go a long way to making him feel more secure and restrict him thrashing his legs up and down, which is one of the main things that causes him to get distressed. Using a pure cotton sheet with a pure cotton cellular blanket is much more effective than just tucking the baby in with a blanket. Rolling up blankets and pushing them down between the spars of the cot and the mattress will also help secure the sheet and blanket. Refer to page 9 for details on how to make up the cot. Once the baby is safely and securely tucked in, I would use the crying down method described on page 39 to allow him to settle himself. In my experience the majority of babies who are well fed and ready to sleep will settle themselves within five or ten minutes, although I have had a few where it took ten to twenty minutes. While it is obviously very distressing to listen to a young baby cry, in my opinion it is prefereable to do this for a few nights than put the baby at risk by laying him on his tummy or side.

It is now commonly regarded that the safest position for your baby to sleep is on his back with his feet at the bottom of the cot so that he cannot wriggle down under the covers. Allowing babies to sleep on their side poses just as great a risk as putting them on their tummy.

*

Ensure that the sheet and blanket are level with his shoulders and are tucked in well, so that the baby cannot pull them over his face. Rolling up blankets and wedging them down either side of your baby could cause over-heating, as can duvets, quilts and pillows. Layers of cotton cellular blankets are best as they can be reduced or increased according to the temperature of the room.

If you are swaddling your baby, use a 100 per cent cotton sheet that has some give in the fabric. Do not double it and make sure that the number of top covers are reduced so that your baby does not get overheated. Once your baby gets to one month start to get him used to being half swaddled so that he is out of his full swaddle by two months.

Once your child reaches six months he may start to roll over on to his tummy and move around the cot. If you have not already done so, it would be safer to put him in a sleeping bag and remove the covers so that he does not get tangle up in them.

The temperature of the room should be maintained at around 18°C (64°F) and not allowed to go below 16°C (61°F) or rise above 20°C (68°F). Using a battery operated room thermometer and thermostatically controlled heating will help ensure that your baby's room is kept at the right temperature. Make sure that the cot is not positioned near a radiator, airing cupboard, chimney-breast or window.

The mattress should conform to British safety standards and be firm, clean and fit properly with no gaps at the sides or the bottom. It should be kept spotlessly clean and aired on a regular basis. In the early days use a draw sheet that tucks in securely over the top of the bottom fitted sheet where your baby's face is, this can be quickly removed and replaced without disturbing your baby too much if he is prone to possetting. Avoid using second hand mattresses. Check regularly that the screws and fittings on the cot have not worked their way loose.

The best way to check your baby's body temperature is by touching his chest with the back of your hand. It is very common for babies to have cold hands and feet so do not use these as a guideline to your baby's body temperature. If the chest does feel too warm, remove a layer of blankets.

Never allow your baby to fall asleep in the house in out-door clothing. Remove hats, mitts and coats when in the house.

Never allow anyone to smoke near your baby or in the rooms in the house frequently used by your baby, and never ever in the baby's room.

Ensure that toddlers, young children and animals are kept out of nursery when your baby is asleep or away from the pram if he is sleeping downstairs. Cats will instinctively curl across a baby's tummy and I know of two very loving toddlers who were caught trying to tuck baby in, unfortunately with a pillow across the baby's face.

Falling asleep on the sofa, particularly while feeding your baby or trying to settle him to sleep is one of the highest risk factors of cot death. If your baby is very unsettled and you are feeling even the slightest bit tired or stressed, it is much safer to put him in his cot for five or ten minutes, while you have a cup of tea and a break to re-charge your batteries. Never feel ashamed to call a friend or a neighbour for help if you are feeling totally exhausted and unable to cope with your baby. It is better than trying to battle on and accidentally falling asleep with your baby in your arms.

For more information on Sudden Infant Death Syndrome contact The Foundation for the Study of Infant Deaths (page 176).

Sleep and darkness

The advice given by the majority of babycare experts on day-time sleep is that the baby should be put to sleep in a light room. This is supposed to help him distinguish between night and day and to sleep better at night. I totally disagree with this theory and believe it is the main cause of catnapping. In order to prevent a baby from developing the habit of catnapping, he must learn to have consolidated blocks of time asleep and time awake. I believe this can only be achieved if the baby learns the difference between awake-time and asleep-time in a dark, quiet room for sleep-time and a bright, noisier room for awake-time.

The following guidelines, together with the routine appropriate to your baby's age, will help you establish the proper quality daytime sleep for your baby, essential for long-term healthy sleep habits.

Curtains

Curtains should be full length and fully lined with black-out lining. It is of the utmost importance that they are fixed to a track that fits flush along the top of the window. Ideally they should have a deep matching pelmet, which is also lined with black-out lining. There should be no gaps between the sides of the curtains and the window frame; even the smallest chink of light can be enough to wake your baby earlier than 7am. For the same reason, curtain poles should be avoided as the light streams out of the gap at the top. As the baby gets older he may not settle back to sleep if woken at 5am by early morning sun or street lights.

I am so convinced that a dark room encourages good sleeping habits that, when I worked as a maternity nurse, I would not take a booking unless the nursery had both curtains with black-out lining and a special black-out rollerblind (see Useful Addresses). When the lights are off and the curtains closed, it should be so dark that you are unable to see your partner standing at the other side of the room. Research has also proved that the chemicals in the brain alter in the dark, conditioning it for sleep. This is one of the reasons why, in the early days, I put my babies in a dark room for all their naps whenever possible.

When to sleep

During the first weeks of life, when a baby sleeps will be very much dictated by when he feeds. Present day trends advocate that young babies should be fed on demand and that their sleep pattern should be allowed to develop naturally. However, over the last few years there has been much research to prove that baby-led feeding does not always lead to happier babies who eventually sleep at the times parents expect them to. The most recent report by Professor Jim

Horne at Loughborough University claims that two-thirds of children aren't getting enough sleep. This lack of sleep is believed to be affecting both the mental and physical development of young children, reducing their alertness and ability to learn. Another recent survey shows that at least a quarter of 10-month-olds were still waking in the night. I am convinced that how much the parents control the times their baby sleeps in the early days will have a huge effect on his long-term sleeping habits.

Over 80 per cent of the calls I now get asking for help are from parents with babies and toddlers aged between nine months and two years. In nearly every case, the cause of the poor sleeping is the baby or toddler being allowed to take the lead with his feeding and sleeping.

Demand feeding and sleeping

My first experience of demand feeding and sleeping is that of my own childhood. As a single parent in the 1950s with no mother of her own to guide her, my mother allowed me to set the pace regarding eating and sleeping. Obviously I cannot remember the very early days, but I can remember as far back as to when I was around 18 months old. I never went to bed until my mother and grandfather did, which according to other members of family was never before midnight.

Certainly I remember that when my mother and I did get into the large double bed we shared sleep did not come naturally. I would play happily with my toys and dollies, who also had to sleep in the bed, while my mother would listen to the blaring music of Mario Lanzio and Elvis. We would eventually drop off to sleep with the music playing and the lights blazing.

In the early days this did not present a problem for either my mother or myself, as we both would sleep very late in the morning. However, when the time came for me to attend school it was a different matter. I remember finding it very difficult to get up in the morning because I was so tired from going to bed so late, and during the years that followed I probably had more sick days off school and spent more time in the sickbay than all the other children put together. I am sure that my teachers will remember me as being a very sickly child, when in fact the only real problem was tiredness.

I believe that lack of sleep during my early years seriously affected my education and I have gone on to have serious sleeping problems all my adult life. In later years I would ask my mother why she didn't have a proper routine and put me to bed earlier. She said that I would get upset and cry and she couldn't bear for me to get distressed. This is a common response from many parents who are experiencing severe problems with older babies and children.

In my experience the very small amount of stress that is involved in sorting out a serious sleep problem is nothing compared to the severe effects that long-term sleep problems have on young children.

My own experience and that of dealing with hundreds of serious sleeping problems over the years has had a profound effect on my approach to dealing with babies and toddlers who experience sleeping difficulties and was a driving force in establishing my own structure for feeding and sleeping.

When used from day one, my routines can establish a healthy sleeping pattern at the right times during the day and ensure that all the needs of a young baby are being met and that the right sleep associations are established from the offset. As thousands of parents will happily testify, this results in a happy, contented baby who will sleep at the right times during the day and sleep through the night from an early age, without the need for any form of sleep-training.

Obviously, getting older babies and toddlers who have developed sleeping problems to sleep well at the right time will probably have to involve some sort of sleep-training alongside the routines. But the advice given in all of my books shows parents how to use these methods to cause the least distress.

The following guidelines as to when you should encourage your baby to sleep during the day will have a big effect on how well he sleeps at night.

The routine

I have tried many different routines over the years and without exception I have found the 7am to 7pm routine to be the one in which tiny babies and young infants are happiest. It fits in with their natural sleep rhythms and their need to feed. I would urge parents to settle their child into the routine outlined in the later chapters of this book that is relevant to their child's age group, as this will ensure the natural development of good sleeping habits. For a chart giving an overview of how the sleep routine progresses during the first three years, see page 37.

Day-time sleep

Allowing too much sleep during the day can result in difficulty in settling in the evening, or in middle of the night wakings. But allowing too little can often result in worse problems. Many parents make the mistake of allowing their baby or toddler little or no sleep during the day in the belief that he will sleep better at night. In my experience this rarely works, as the baby or toddler usually becomes so over-tired and irritable that he is difficult to settle in the evening and is much more likely to wake up in the night.

Research confirms what I have always believed. Poor quality day-time sleep can affect not only the baby's mental development but also his ability to sleep well at night. Dr Marc Weissbluth, a leading researcher, paediatrician and director of the Sleep Disorders Center, Children's Memorial Hospital, Chicago, has conducted extensive research into the nap patterns of more than 200 children. In his book *Healthy Sleep Habits, Happy Child* he says that: 'Napping is one of the health habits that sets the stage for good overall sleep.' He explains that a nap offers the baby or child a break from stimuli and allows it to recharge for further activity. Several other experts are in agreement that naps are essential to a baby's brain development and to helping establish long-term healthy sleep patterns.

John Herman, PhD, infant sleep expert and associate professor of psychology and psychiatry at the University of Texas, says: 'If activities are being scheduled to the detriment of sleep, it's a mistake. Parents should remember that everything else in a baby's life should come after sleeping and eating.' Charles Schaefer, PhD, professor of psychology at Fairleigh Dickinson University in Teaneck, New Jersey, supports this research and says: 'Naps structure the day, shape both the baby's and the mother's moods and offer the only opportunity for Mum to relax or accomplish a few tasks.'

There is further evidence to support my view of the importance of day-time sleep being established at the right time. The best time for the biggest nap of the day is between 12 noon and 2pm since this coincides with the baby's natural dip in alertness. A nap at this time will be deeper and more refreshing than a nap that starts later in the day.

Although babies and toddlers do vary in the amount of sleep they require, it is important that you have a clear understanding of how much sleep they need. The following summary of day-time sleep is a guide to how much sleep your baby or toddler needs and the best times for sleep to happen.

Summary of day-time sleep between 7am and 7pm

Morning Nap

A baby under one month of age is usually ready for a nap 1½ hours from the time he wakes in the morning. By the time babies reach two months of age most will manage to stay awake the full two hours. If a baby stays awake longer than two hours he will often become over-tired and fight sleep. Over-tiredness is one of the main causes of very young babies not settling well at nap-time, and care should be taken that this does not happen. By the time they reach six months the majority of babies can stay awake for nearly 2½ hours. All babies should be woken no later than 10am if you want them to sleep for a longer time at 12 noon.

At around one year of age most babies will cut right back on their morning nap, usually cutting it out altogether somewhere between 15 and 18 months.

Lunchtime nap

A baby under one month is often ready for this nap around 11.30am, but by the time he reaches two months he can usually make it to 12 noon. Ideally, this should be the biggest nap of the day, as research shows that a nap between 12 noon and 2pm is deeper and more refreshing than a later nap, because it coincides with the baby's natural dip in alertness. Once a baby reaches six months of age and his morning nap becomes later, the lunchtime nap will also come later – usually around 12.30pm

I have observed that between six and nine months many babies who have slept regularly to 7am will often start to wake up earlier in the morning if the parents have not pushed the morning and lunchtime nap on to 9.30am and 12.30pm.

Depending on how well the baby has slept in the morning nap, this nap usually lasts between 2 and 2½ hours. At around one year of age this may be cut back to 1½ hours if the baby is still having a full 45-minute nap in the morning, although it may lengthen again to two hours if the morning nap is cut right back or dropped altogether. The majority of babies will continue to need a nap at midday until they are two years of age, at which time they will gradually reduce the amount of time they sleep, cutting it out altogether between two and a half and three years of age.

Late-afternoon nap

If a baby sleeps well at the two earlier naps of the day, this should be the shortest of the three naps. A baby under eight weeks usually needs between 30 minutes and one hour. By the time they reach 12 weeks of age the majority of babies who have slept well at lunchtime will only need a very short nap of 15–20 minutes, in order to revive them enough for the bath and bedtime routine.

This nap is usually dropped somewhere between three and six months of age. Allowing a baby to have a longer sleep later in the day is often the reason a baby does not settle well at 7pm.

The total amount of daily sleep your baby or toddler has between 7am and 7pm will play a big part in how well he sleeps at night. The timing of the sleep is also important if over-tiredness is to be avoided. Listed below is an approximate guide to the number of hours of nap-time a baby or toddler needs.

- Birth to four weeks – 5 hours
- Four to eight weeks – 4 to 4½ hours
- Eight to 12 weeks – 3½ hours
- Three to six months – 3 hours
- Six to 12 months – 2½ to 3 hours
- 12 to 15 months – 2½ hours
- 15 to 18 months – 2 to 2½ hours
- 18 to 24 months – 2 hours
- Two years to two and a half years – 1 to 2 hours
- Two and a half to three years – 0 to 1 hour

How to sleep

Through all my experience of working with children I have come to the conclusion that the key to ensuring good sleeping habits is teaching your baby or child to go to sleep in his cot/bed unassisted. Establishing the right sleep associations from an early age is vital if you wish to avoid long-term sleep problems.

Sleep associations

If you constantly cuddle, rock, feed or use the dummy to get your baby to sleep, it is what he will come to associate with falling asleep. This does not often create a problem during the first few weeks, but once the baby develops and starts to come into a light sleep every 40–50 minutes, a real problem can evolve. In my experience babies who depend on their parents to help them get to sleep will, at around eight to 12 weeks, start to wake up increasingly in the night. Babies who were often feeding only once in the night end up feeding every couple of hours; others will not settle unless cuddled or rocked, or given the dummy.

If your baby is under eight weeks, this problem can be avoided by ensuring that you allow enough time to settle your baby at sleep-times. Make a note of how long your baby can stay awake before he falls asleep then make sure that you allow a 10- or 15-minute wind down period before he goes to sleep. If he has fed earlier and is unsettled but you are sure he is not hungry or windy, give him a cuddle or the dummy, but make sure that he is settled in his cot before he falls asleep and without the dummy. If he has just had a feed and is falling asleep on the breast or bottle, try to arouse him slightly before you put him into the cot so that he is aware that he is going into his cot.

Provided he has been well fed and winded and is ready to sleep, he should drift off to sleep within five to ten minutes, although I have had a few babies who would fuss and fret for up to 20 minutes before settling off to sleep. If your baby is under eight weeks and not settling well despite looking sleepy, it is important that you look closely at his feeding. In my experience the cause is usually one of two things: the baby is still hungry or the baby was too sleepy during the feed and is not quite ready to settle.

With an older baby or toddler who doesn't know how to go to sleep unassisted, eliminating the wrong sleep associations will be more difficult and some form of sleep-training (refer to page 38) will probably be needed if persistent night-time wakings are to be resolved and a healthy sleeping pattern established.

Establishing healthy sleeping habits also depends on several other factors. Getting the feeding right and ensuring that your baby or toddler's physical, mental and emotional needs are being met also have a huge influence on how well he sleeps.

The bedtime routine

The majority of experts agree that a good bedtime routine is important for young babies and children. However, there is much disagreement over the age at which parents should start a bedtime routine and what it should consist of. Somewhere between the age of six weeks and three months seems to be the time that most experts think you can start to establish regular times for a bath, feed and then settling the baby in its bed.

My own view, based on caring for hundreds of babies, is that the sooner a bedtime routine is established, the less likely the parents are to encounter problems trying to settle their baby. A baby of six weeks will more than likely create a fuss if you suddenly try to settle him in his nursery by himself in the evening, and a baby of three months even more so. If they have been used to sleeping on and off in their bouncy chair or Moses basket in the living room, they will certainly have got used to falling asleep with the lights on and amongst noise. A pattern of catnapping will very quickly become established, and in my opinion that makes it more difficult when, weeks down the line, parents decide that they want to establish a bedtime routine. When I worked as a maternity nurse I established a routine in the very early days, usually around the fifth day, when the mother's milk has come in. I believe that this is one of the reasons I rarely had to deal with a crying baby in the evening.

Of course there are times in the early days when the young baby will not immediately fall asleep, but if you are consistent in how you try to settle him, a pattern should very quickly emerge where he settles quickly and easily, between 6.30 and 7pm in the evening. This will have a knock-on effect on what happens later and in the middle of the night. A baby who feeds and settles well in the early evening and sleeps until his next feed is due is much more likely to feed well at the last feed of the night, which should come at around 10 or 11pm.

This is particularly true of breast fed babies, as the time the baby sleeps in the evening allows the mother to have a meal and a good rest, which will help ensure that she has time to produce enough milk for a good feed last thing at night. A baby who has a good last feed is much more likely only to wake up once in the night and then settle quickly, because again the mother will have had sufficient rest to produce enough milk for a full feed.

Regardless of whether he is bottle fed or breast fed, if a baby gets into the habit of catnapping in the early evening, he will more than likely get into the habit of feeding little and often. When the parents attempt to feed him before they go to bed, it is very unlikely that he will take a full feed, particularly if he has fed within the last couple of hours. He will therefore be much more likely to wake up around 1am looking for a feed, then again at 5am. A pattern of two feeds a night is very quickly established, and for a breast feeding mother this can have dire consequences as tiredness sets in and the milk supply is greatly reduced.

If you wish to avoid a pattern of unsettled evenings and excessive waking in the middle of the night, I would strongly advise that you establish a routine as soon as possible.

Bathtime

I am aware that many experts advise that it is not necessary to bathe your baby every day and that a top and tail will suffice in the early days.

I believe that babies are no different from us adults and that a warm bath and a gentle massage is a wonderful way of unwinding and relaxing in the evening. Recent research also claims that babies who are bathed and massaged in the evening tend to sleep better than those that aren't. The following guidelines will help ensure that bathtime is a calm and relaxing occasion.

Never attempt to bath a baby who is tired, hungry and getting near his feed time. Until they are near eight weeks, split the feed. Give him half of his feed after he has had a short nap late-afternoon, around 5pm. Allow a good 45 minutes before beginning the bath.

Prepare everything in advance for the bath, making sure that you have towels, nightclothes, creams and everything else needed laid out ready.

Close the curtains in the bedroom and lower the lighting. Make sure that the bedroom and bathroom are warm enough. Very young babies feel the cold more than adults and you may have to put the heating on for a short spell on a cold day in the spring or summer.

When you lower your baby into the bath, remember that he can only see a distance of 8 to 12 inches. Try to position the bath and yourself so that he has close contact with you and doesn't lose sight of your face.

Make sure that the water is warm enough but not too hot. Once your baby is in the bath he may thrash his arms and get upset. Holding both his hands across his chest with one of your hands will help him calm down. This is easier to do if he is lying on a special bath support within the bath. These are usually made of towelling attached to a frame or a specially moulded piece of foam or plastic.

Settling a baby of under six weeks

The following guidelines will be of help when trying to settle a baby at bedtime.

- In order for a small baby to settle well in the evening it is very important that he takes a full feed prior to going to bed, is well winded and has been awake enough throughout the day and is ready to sleep.

- Babies under six weeks can usually stay awake for between one and two hours at a time. A baby who has only been awake a total of four hours between 7am and 7pm may not settle as quickly as a baby who has been awake a total of six hours.

- Keep a diary of what your baby takes at each feed during the day and how long he is awake, then if he is unsettled you may be able to trace why from your notes.

- Keep the bedtime routine calm and quiet; once the bath is over, do not allow lots of visitors in the nursery as this can over-stimulate the baby.

- Keep the lights dim and avoid lots of talking and eye contact during the last feed. Make sure that he is well winded before you attempt to settle him in his cot.

- Always settle your baby in his cot before he falls asleep. If he has become sleepy on the breast or bottle, rouse him slightly before putting him in the cot.

• Make sure that he is tucked in very securely, as babies under six weeks still have a strong Moro reflex and get very upset when they thrash their arms and legs around. Some younger or smaller babies may benefit from swaddling.

Try to allow your baby five to ten minutes to settle himself to sleep. If he is getting very upset, pick him up and offer him more to eat. Hunger is one of the main causes of young babies not settling in the evening, particularly breast fed babies. Resettle him in his cot again and leave him a further five or ten minutes, if he is still very unsettled, repeat the same procedure. You may find that for the first few nights you have to resettle him several times before he eventually falls asleep.

The important thing is to be consistent and persistent. In the long-term this will be much more reassuring to your baby than to keep changing your tactic at bedtime. Do not be tempted to take him downstairs into his day-time environment, as this will confuse him even more.

If, after several nights, you find that it is taking many attempts to settle him and you are convinced that he is well fed and winded and has been awake enough and is ready to sleep, try sitting or lying quietly with him in the darkened room for a few nights. If you find that he will fall asleep in your arms happily for over an hour or more but get upset when put in the cot, it may be that he has already learned some of the wrong sleep associations. You will then have to decide whether you are going to continue to establish the wrong sleep associations by assisting him to sleep or use the crying down method (see page 39) to help him learn how to settle himself to sleep.

Establishing a bedtime routine for an older baby or toddler

If you have not already established a bedtime routine, follow the guidelines recommended above, but do so an hour prior to the time your baby or toddler is going to bed at present. After several nights of following the bathtime routine you can then gradually start to move it forward 10 or 20 minutes every few nights, until you reach the time you have decided that you want your baby or toddler to go to bed. Obviously if your baby or toddler is not sleeping well at night, then you would probably have to implement some sort of sleep-training, but this should only be done once you are confident that you are getting his feeding right during the day. Attempting to sleep train a baby or toddler who is not getting enough to eat at the right times during the day would more than likely end in failure.

Sleep inhibitors

There are many factors that can prevent babies and children from sleeping well and it is important to ensure that none of these are having an effect on your child. Below is a brief introduction to each of the main sleep inhibitors.

Hunger

Ensuring that your baby or toddler is receiving a correct, nutritionally balanced diet during the day is very important. In the very early days it is important that the baby does not need to wake up for extra food or drinks in the night because he is not getting what he needs during the day. Often I speak to parents of older babies who are still waking and feeding two or three times a night simply because they are not getting enough to eat during the day. By the time they reach nine months a vicious circle has been established. The baby will not eat enough during the day because he is having milk during the night and he will not sleep at night without the milk because he has not had enough to eat during the day.

I have seen this problem go on well into toddlerhood and it is one of the main reasons why I am in favour of structuring milk feeds from the very early days. I believe that the term 'demand feeding' is one of the main causes of sleeping problems. In the early days it leads parents to believe that every time their baby cries it must be hunger and therefore not to look at other reasons for the crying. It

Milk feeding chart for the first year

Age	Times
2–4 weeks	2–3am 6–7am 10–10.30am 2–2.30am 5pm 6–6.30pm 10–11pm
4–6 weeks	3–4am 6–7am 10.30–am 2–2.30pm 5pm 6–6.30pm 10–11pm
6–8 weeks	4–5am 730am 10.45 am 2–2.30pm 6–6.30pm 10–11pm
8–10 weeks	5–6am 730am 11am 2–2.30pm 6–6.30pm 10–11pm
10–12 weeks	7am 11am 2–2.30pm 6–6.30pm 10–11pm
3–4 months	7am 11am 2–2.30pm 6–6.30pm 10–10.30pm
4–5 months	7am 11am 2–2.30pm 6–6.30pm 10pm
5–6 months	7am 11.30am 2–2.30pm 6–6.30pm
6–7 months	7am 2–2.30pm 6–6.30pm
7–8 months	7am 2–2.30pm 6–6.30pm
8–9 months	7am 2–2.30pm 6–6.30pm
9–10 months	7am 5pm 6.30–7pm
10–12 months	7am 5pm 6.30–7pm

more often than not results in the baby continuing to feed little and often long after the time when he is capable of taking a bigger milk feed and sleeping a longer stretch in the night.

Obviously, young babies must never be made to wait for food when they are hungry but it is also important that you understand your baby or child's nutritional needs and that you structure their daily intake according to their age.

Diet

Certain foods and drinks can affect the sleep of young babies and toddlers. Breast feeding mothers should avoid alcohol, artificial sweeteners, excess caffeine and highly spiced foods. Caffeine is present in tea, chocolate and some soft drinks as well as coffee. I have also found that some babies react very badly if their mothers have eaten strawberries, tomatoes, mushrooms or onions in large quantities, or drunk excessive amounts of fruit juice. It is essential to eat a healthy varied diet while breast feeding; therefore I do not suggest that you cut out everything mentioned above. But if your baby is prone to waking up several times a night for reasons other than hunger, it may be that something you have eaten or drunk is affecting him. Keeping a food diary for a week may help you to find out if there is a link between disturbed nights and eating certain foods. You should also monitor your dairy intake, as some research links dairy products colic.

During the early days of weaning it is also advisable to keep a diary of what foods your baby eats and any reactions he has. The most common foods that I have found can cause waking in the nights with babies under six months are bananas, citrus fruits, tomatoes, sweet potatoes and carrots given in excessive amounts. Again I am not suggesting that you eliminate these from your baby's diet, but keeping a detailed food diary alongside your sleeping diary will help you spot any offending foods.

With older babies and toddlers I am convinced that too much processed food high in sugar and additives can cause poor night-time sleep. Too many sweets and chocolates certainly affect the behaviour and sleep of some toddlers, as do excessive amounts of fruit juices and squashes.

Over-tiredness

If a baby or toddler becomes over-tired either physically or men-tally, he will become very irritable and stressed. I believe that over-tiredness is another major reason why many babies and young children do not settle to sleep easily in the evening and wake up several times a night.

Many babies and toddlers do not give off an obvious signal of tiredness and are allowed to stay awake for too long a period between day-time naps. Others are kept up too late in the evening by their parents in the hope that they will sleep better in the night. In both cases the baby or toddler becomes over-tired, fussy and fretful and fights sleep. Parents, desperate to help their child get some much-needed sleep, often resort to feeding, rocking or giving the dummy. A double problem of over-tiredness and the wrong sleep associations is quickly established.

By ensuring that you structure his social time to fit in with your baby's sleeping and feeding needs, over-tiredness can be avoided. Check the required sleep needed and the times for your baby or toddler's age to ensure that you are not allowing him to become over-tired.

Over-stimulation

Over-stimulation prior to sleep-time is another main of cause of babies and children not settling and sleeping well. Over-handling prior to sleep-time can cause real problems with babies under six months.

Everyone wants just one little cuddle before bedtime. Unfortunately, several little cuddles from several different people all add up, and can leave your baby fretful, over-tired and difficult to settle. Please, do not feel guilty about restricting the handling during the first few months, especially prior to sleep-times. Allow a quiet wind down period of 15–20 minutes before naps or bedtime, and avoid lots of talking and eye contact. This will become a signal to your baby that it is quiet time and prepare him for sleep.

With older babies and toddlers, after the bath keep things very calm and talk quietly using simple phases. Do not get into long-winded conversations at this stage and avoid games and activities that could cause them to become over-excited.

Wind

If a baby is not properly winded he may experience serious discomfort when put down to sleep. It is therefore essential to eliminate wind as the cause of crying and sleeplessness. I would advise following your baby's lead regarding when to stop and wind him. If you constantly interrupt his feed to get his wind up, he will be likely to get so upset and frustrated that the crying will cause more wind than the feed itself. The reality is that very few babies need to be burped more than once during a feed and once at the end. A baby who is genuinely bothered by wind will scream and scream after a feed – nothing will console him until he manages to burp. Please see the section on wind on page 61 for further information.

Illness

A baby under three months of age will usually need help to get through the night when he has a cold or is ill. A young baby with a cold can get very distressed, especially when he is feeding, as he will not have learned to breathe through his mouth. If your baby develops a cold or cough, regardless how mild it appears, he should be seen by a doctor.

All too often I hear from distressed parents of babies with serious chest infections, which possibly could have been avoided if they had been seen by a doctor earlier. Too many mothers delay taking their baby to the doctor, worried that they be classed as neurotic, but it is important that you discuss with your doctor any concerns you have about your baby's health, no matter how small. If your baby is ill, it is essential that your follow to the letter your doctor's advice, especially on feeding.

Anxiety

By the age of six months, babies begin to realise they are separate from their mothers and a baby may show signs of separation anxiety or stranger anxiety. The happy contented baby who was so easy-going and relaxed and who would go to anyone suddenly becomes clingy, anxious and demanding.

He screams if his mother leaves the room for even a few minutes and often gets hysterical if approached by a stranger. Some babies will even get upset when relations they know well attempt to talk to them or pick them up. This behaviour is a totally normal part of the baby's development. All babies go through this stage to some degree between the age of six and 12 months, and it is usually around nine months that it becomes most obvious. In my experience, babies who are used to being with someone else on a regular basis usually suffer less from separation anxiety.

If your baby suddenly becomes more clingy around this age it is important to understand that he is not being naughty or demanding. Forcing him to go to strangers or leaving him alone in a room to play by himself will not solve the problem and may lead to him become more fretful and insecure. Because this stage often coincides with the time a mother returns to work, a baby who has always slept well at night can start to wake up in the night fretful and anxious. Responding quickly and positively to his anxiety rather than ignoring it will, in the long run, help him to become more confident and independent. However, it is important that you do not allow your baby to feel that he is being rewarded for his night-time waking by giving him too much attention.

Please see page 108 for further information.

Teething

In my experience, babies who enjoy a routine from a very early age and have established healthy sleeping habits are rarely bothered by teething. I have found that babies who have suffered from colic or have developed poor sleeping habits are more likely to wake in the night when they are teething. However, some babies who normally sleep well do wake up for a short spell when the molars are coming through.

If you are convinced that your baby's night-time wakings are caused by severe teething pain, I suggest you seek advice from your doctor regarding the use of paracetamol. While genuine teething pain may cause a few disruptive nights, it should never last for several weeks.

If your baby is teething and waking in the night but quickly settles back to sleep when given a cuddle or a dummy, teething is probably not the real cause of the waking. A baby who is genuinely bothered by teething pain would be difficult to settle back to sleep. He would also show signs of discomfort during the day, not just at night.

Discomfort

Ensuring that your baby or toddler is comfortable is essential when establishing good sleep habits. Getting the room temperature right so that he is neither too hot nor too cold is very important, as is dressing him in comfortable clothing for sleeping. Please refer to pages 4–5 and 8–9 for further information on making up a cot and room temperature.

Nappy rash

When choosing disposable nappies it is worthwhile buying one of the more expensive brands, which in my experience are much more absorbent than some of the cheaper ones. A good quality disposable nappy and regular nappy changes should ensure that nappy rash is avoided. However, some babies and toddlers do have very sensitive skin. Should yours develop nappy rash it could cause him to be very unsettled, as the red or broken skin can be extremely painful, particularly when it comes into contact with urine or stools. If your baby or toddler's bottom does become affected you will need to change his nappies even more frequently than usual. Using an unperfumed baby oil and cotton wool to clean the sensitive area will be less painful than using water or baby wipes. If you are using terry nappies it is worthwhile considering putting your baby in disposable nappies for nap-times until the rash clears up. Frequent changing and cleaning and the use of a good quality barrier cream at every nappy change should clear the rash up within a few days. A rash that persists after a few days should be seen by a doctor as it may be a candidal rash, often referred to as thrush, which will need a special anti-fungal cream.

The following guidelines, if followed to the letter, should help avoid nappy rash with even the most sensitive skinned baby or toddler:

- Check and change your baby or toddler's nappy every couple of hours regardless of whether he has had a bowel movement.

- Clean your baby or toddler's bottom with either cool boiled water or unperfumed baby oil and cotton wool. Avoid using baby wipes on very young babies, especially if the bottom area looks red, as the perfume they contain can sometimes cause irritation.

- If you use a barrier cream, apply only a thin layer. Too much will reduce the absorbency of disposable nappies. Never use baby powder as it can clog the baby's skin and even the tiniest amount can prove fatal if it reaches a baby's lungs.

- Remove your baby or toddler's nappy and expose his bottom to fresh air at least twice a day.

2
Solutions For
Sleepless Nights

Sleepless nights – the cause

Every month I am contacted by hundreds of parents asking for advice about their baby or toddler's sleeping habits. Most of these parents were following the current advice of feeding the baby on demand and allowing him to find his own sleeping pattern. They trusted the advice that it is impossible to implement a routine for a baby under three months and that by feeding him on demand he will eventually find his own sleeping pattern naturally. While many babies do fall into a routine of their own accord and will sleep through the night from an early age, in my experience the majority do not.

If I needed further evidence of the seriousness of the epidemic of sleep problems at present, the response to articles in the *Daily Telegraph* and *Evening Standard* provides powerful proof. Phone lines were jammed for several days by thousands of parents wanting to order *The Contented Little Baby Book*.

Critics of my routines remain adamant that it is natural for young babies to wake up several times a night and parents must accept sleep deprivation as normal. Such is the lack of support from health officials for parents wanting routine that a huge number have set about organising their own support groups. These parents all share a common belief – that babies and young children are happier and sleep better when in a routine.

Dr Brian Synon, a senior lecturer in general practice at the

University of Adelaide also shares my belief that parents should strive towards developing a routine during the first six weeks. He also stresses the importance of monitoring day-time sleep to ensure that the long stretch of sleep is at night. In his book *Silent Nights* he says that a baby between six and seven weeks who is feeding and growing well is able to sleep at night for one long block of sleep of seven hours after the last feed. By eight weeks this can be extended to eight hours. Between three and six months he says most babies are capable of sleeping 7pm–7am, although some may need to feed briefly at the parents' bedtime.

Although babies and toddlers do vary in the amount of sleep they require, it is important that you have a clear understanding of how much sleep your baby needs. The following chart can be used as a guide to how much sleep your baby or toddler should get and the best times for sleep to happen. This will help you determine whether your baby or toddler is waking excessively in the night.

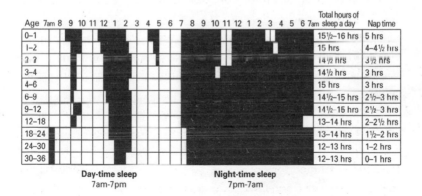

Age	Total hours of sleep a day	Nap time
0–1	15½–16 hrs	5 hrs
1–2	15 hrs	4–4½ hrs
2–3	14½ hrs	3½ hrs
3–4	14½ hrs	3 hrs
4–6	15 hrs	3 hrs
6–9	14½–15 hrs	2½–3 hrs
9–12	14½–16 hrs	2½–3 hrs
12–18	13–14 hrs	2–2½ hrs
18–24	13–14 hrs	1½–2 hrs
24–30	12–13 hrs	1–2 hrs
30–36	12–13 hrs	0–1 hrs

Day-time sleep 7am-7pm Night-time sleep 7pm-7am

How you deal with excessive night-time waking will depend very much on the age of your baby or toddler and the reason for their waking. Babies or toddlers who are in the habit of waking several times a night and need assistance to get back to sleep will eventually grow out of the habit, but this rarely happens before the age of about three years. If you wish to resolve the problem sooner, you will need to resort to some form of sleep-training. For sleep-training to be successful, the baby or child must learn to settle themselves back to sleep, without any help from the parents.

Sleep-training – preparation

Sleep-training can be both mentally and emotionally draining for parents and it is not something that should be started without considerable thought. If you decide to sleep-train your baby or child, it is essential that your baby or child has a medical check-up with your doctor, so that he can confirm that there are no medical reasons why you should not attempt sleep-training. It is also worthwhile seeking advice and support from your health visitor, who may be able to put you in touch with your nearest sleep clinic.

For sleep-training to be successful it is important that you can commit at least two weeks of your time to resolving the problem. Sleep-training should not be attempted under any of the following circumstances:

- Your baby is not gaining weight. A baby not gaining weight should always be seen by a doctor. Sleep-training should only be used if your baby is regularly gaining a good amount of weight each week. Babies under four months should be gaining an average of 6–8oz each week and babies aged four to six months should be gaining an average of 4–8oz each week.

- Your baby or toddler is just recovering from an illness, or any other member of the family is unwell.

- You are about to move home, go on holiday or have visitors to stay within the next two weeks.

- Any younger or older siblings are going through a difficult time either mentally, physically or emotionally, or about to start nursery or pre-school.

- Your baby or toddler has just started or is about to start nursery or pre-school.

- Either you or your partner is under pressure at work.

It is also important that the same person deals with the baby throughout the sleep-training. It can be very confusing for the baby or child when a different parent keeps appearing at different times during the night.

Sleeping through the night from an early age

With babies under six months, excessive wakings in the night are often due to hunger. Therefore, before attempting any of the following programmes I would advise that you follow a strict routine of feeding and sleeping as outlined in this book. For many parents, following the routines to the letter will automatically resolve the problem.

Your baby must take full milk feeds at the times stated, eating enough solids, if they are weaned and be awake for most of the recommended times and if they are to settle well. Provided they have not learned any of the wrong sleep associations, they should settle to sleep with the minimum of fuss, in say five to ten minutes. If they become over-tired or tend to fight sleep, then crying down could be used.

If a baby of under six months has learned to go to sleep at the wrong times or will only sleep when rocked or held, he should be put on the routine appropriate for his age, but for several days assisted to sleep in the usual way. This will help his body clock become used to sleeping at the times on the routine. Once this has happened, then he can be put in his cot and crying down can be used to settle him to sleep. If he is over eight weeks, gaining weight well and still feeding more than once in the middle of the night, then the core night method can be used.

Crying down (birth to six months)

Crying down can be particularly helpful when feeding problems have been resolved and a baby or toddler has only mild sleep association problems or has difficulty falling asleep because he is over-tired or over-stimulated. Dr Brian Symon uses this term to describe the pattern of crying when an over-tired baby is going to sleep. Crying down, he says, is the reverse of crying up, crying up being the description of a baby waking up from a good sleep and starting to demand a feed. Crying up starts with silence. The baby is asleep, he wakes. His first sounds are soft, gentle, subtle. After a minute or two of being ignored, the baby begins to cry. He will cry for a short spell, then go quiet for a short spell. If he is ignored, the crying starts again but louder. Crying gradually increases in volume, with the gaps between cries becoming shorter until the baby is emitting a continuous loud bellow.

Crying down, is the reverse of that picture. The over-tired baby will start to bellow loudly when put down to sleep and the reverse pattern begins. The process of crying down to sleep takes between 10 and 30 minutes. The more over-tired the baby is, the louder and longer he will cry. Dr Symon stresses that this technique will only work if the baby is allowed to settle himself to sleep. Parents who find the crying difficult to ignore are advised to wait 10 minutes before going in to him. They can then enter and reassure the baby with a soothing touch or quiet voice.

Reassurance must be kept to a maximum of one to two minutes. Parents should then wait a further 10–15 minutes before returning. For this technique to work it is essential that the baby is not picked up and that he is allowed to settle by himself in his cot.

Dr Symon believes that parents who do not allow their over-tired baby to get himself off to sleep are creating long-term sleep problems. His beliefs have recently been confirmed by research at Oxford University. They conclude that a 20-minute 'winding down' bedtime routine, coupled with ignoring crying for gradually increasing intervals, is an effective way of dealing with babies and children who resist sleep.

Provided a baby has been well fed and is ready to sleep, I believe he should be allowed to settle himself. The above method works not only for over-tired babies but also for babies who fight sleep. Although it is very difficult to listen to a young baby cry himself to sleep, it will prevent serious sleep problems in the future. Parents who are not prepared to leave their baby to cry for 10–20 minutes usually end up resorting to feeding, rocking or giving a dummy to induce sleep. This can often take up to two hours, resulting in exhausted parents and the baby waking up when he comes into his light sleep looking for the same inducement to get back to sleep again.

It is my belief that, in the long-term, allowing your baby to develop the wrong sleep associations and therefore denying him the sound night's sleep he needs in order to develop both mentally and physically is a worse option than hearing him cry for a short while. Allowing your baby to learn to go to sleep unassisted is your aim, and it is important to remember that this will prevent much greater upset and more crying if waking in the night is due to your baby not knowing how to go back to sleep after having woken in light sleep.

Filmed research shows that all babies come into a light sleep several times a night. Some will even wake up briefly before drifting back to sleep. Babies who have learned the wrong sleep associations will be unable to get back to sleep unaided, and will need whatever methods the parents use to assist them to sleep, be it feeding, rocking or the dummy. Some babies may need all three comforts before dropping back off to sleep. These babies are very unlikely to learn to sleep through the night and usually continue to wake up several times a night.

Crying down with a baby under six weeks usually lasts between five and ten minutes, although with some babies who have become over-tired and fight sleep it can last up to 20 minutes. Provided all the baby's needs have been met, he will normally learn how to settle himself to sleep within a few nights, although some babies do continue to cry down at bedtime for several weeks. However, the time they cry does usually get progressively less.

If you are breast feeding, I would always advise that you offer your baby a top-up of expressed milk before attempting crying down, to be 100 per cent sure that hunger is not the reason he is not settling.

The Core Night (for babies over six weeks and weighing more than 10lb)

The core night method can be used for a baby over six weeks who weighs more than 10lb and is following the contented little baby routines to the letter, and provided he is putting on enough weight each week. You will know it is the right time to start thinking about this method when your baby is still waking in the night looking for a feed, but not feeding well at 7am.

The method can also be used to lengthen the time between feeds of babies from six weeks old who continue to wake up at 2am out of habit, take only a small amount to eat, then wake up again at 5am – provided they are achieving a good weight gain. The aim here is to eliminate one of the night feeds so that the baby feeds better at the second waking. It is not to push the baby through the night without any feed at all.

The 'core night' is a name that has been used for many years by some maternity nurses and parents who believe in routine. It works on the principle that once a baby sleeps for one longer spell in the night, he should never again be fed during the hours slept in the course of the core night. Once you have seen that your baby can last a certain length of time without a feed, you should use this moment as a window of opportunity to help him to continue to sleep longer. If he wakes during those hours, he should be left for a few minutes to settle himself back to sleep. If he refuses to settle, then other methods than feeding should be used to settle him. Hollyer and Smith recommend patting, offering him a dummy or giving him a sip of water. Attention should be kept to the minimum while reassuring the baby you are there. They claim that following this approach will, within days, have your baby sleeping at least the hours of his first core night. It also teaches the baby the two most important sleeping skills: how to go to sleep, and how to go back to sleep after surfacing from a non-REM (rapid eye movement) sleep.

Dr Brian Symon, author of *Silent Nights* and a senior lecturer in general practice at the University of Adelaide, recommends a similar approach for babies over six weeks. Babies who are putting on a good amount of weight each week, but who are still waking at 3am should be offered the dummy or some cool boiled water. If the baby refuses to settle, then give the shortest possible feed that will allow him to settle.

Neither of these methods of dealing with night feeding are new in baby care. London-based baby care expert Christine Bruell, who has advised over 35,000 mothers during her 40-year career, also advises offering cool boiled water to a thriving baby over four weeks of age if he regularly wakes at 2am. If your baby is under three months, it is important to increase the length of time your baby can go from his last feed gradually and not attempt to eliminate the middle of the night feed in one go.

This method can also be used to try to reduce the number of times a demand-fed baby is fed in the night and to encourage a longer stretch between feeds. But, again, things should be done gradually, working towards eliminating one feed at a time. Attempting to eliminate two or three feeds in one night will lead to a very distressing night for both you and your baby.

Before embarking on these methods, the following points should be read carefully to make sure that your baby really is capable of going for a longer spell in the night.

- It is important to ensure that your baby's last feed is substantial enough to help him sleep for a longer stretch in the night. The majority of babies still need a fifth feed until they are nearly five months old, and some babies who are exclusively breast fed may not drop their fifth feed until they are nearer six months.

- The main sign that a baby is ready to cut down and drop the middle of the night feed is a regular weight gain and a reluctance to feed, or feeding less at 7am.

- The aim of using any of the above methods is gradually to increase the length of time your baby can go from his last feed and not to eliminate the middle of the night feed in one go.

- This method can work particularly well with babies under six months by getting them to feed less and less in the night, gradually dropping the middle of the night feeding. It can also work well in getting rid of night-time feedings with older babies and toddlers, but with these some degree of controlled crying may be necessary if an association problem has set in.

- The core night can also be used with babies between four and six months who are weaned and still waking up in the night looking for a milk feed.

Older babies and toddlers who are still feeding and waking in the night and have learned the wrong sleep associations can be prepared for controlled crying by using the core night. Once they are down to one milk feed in the night, this can gradually be diluted until they are taking only water. Once the parents have arrived at this stage, then they can use controlled crying.

Diluting feeds (babies and toddlers over 6 months)

Before considering this method I urge parents to return to the preparation for sleep-training section. It is important to note that this method should only be used if you have first consulted with a medical professional and your baby is over six months and has had his weight checked.

Diluting feeds is often recommended as a way of eliminating excessive night-time feeding with babies over six months and toddlers. The reason that many parents have problems with this method of eliminating night feeding is because a vicious circle has evolved in which the baby or toddler does not eat enough during the day and is therefore genuinely hungry in the night. When the parents attempt to dilute the feed each time the baby or toddler wakes, he will often settle at the first waking but not at the next or subsequent wakings. In my experience it works best if feeds are eliminated one at time. If your baby or toddler is waking up two or three times a night and you attempt to dilute each feed, you will more than likely be up all night with a very disgruntled baby or toddler.

Start off by gradually diluting the first feed of the night. Whatever your baby or toddler normally takes, dilute it by 30ml (1oz). For example 180ml (6oz) of water and only five scoops of formula, or 150ml (5oz) of full-fat cows' milk and 30ml (1oz) of water. Each night dilute it by a further 30ml (1oz) until the feed comprises only 30ml (1oz) of milk and the rest water. Do not worry at this stage if your toddler actually drinks more the next time he wakes, as the first stage of this plan is to eliminate the number of feeds he is having. Once he has been having the very dilute feed for a couple of nights, you should then attempt to settle him with just plain water. Even if it takes an hour or so, it is important not to give in at this first waking and go back to feeding him.

Once you have managed to settle him at the first waking without feeding him for several nights, you can then start to eliminate the next feed in the same way. If you have noticed an increase in his day-time eating and feeding, you can start off by eliminating the next feed by 50 per cent. Within three or four nights you should be settling him at this waking with only water, and then by any other means than a drink. Any other feeds should be eliminated in exactly the same way. Once you are down to one diluted feed, in the night, you can attempt controlled crying with confidence, knowing that your baby or toddler is not waking up genuinely hungry in the night.

With babies who are drinking excessive milk during the day and refusing solids, I would advise discussing things with your health visitor or doctor first.

Controlled crying (babies and toddlers over six months)

With babies between six months and one year of age, waking in the night is often due to a mixture of hunger and association, caused by a lack of structure in the baby's feeding and sleeping. If a baby or toddler has learned the wrong sleep associations and needs to be rocked, cuddled or fed to sleep, then it is inevitable that some degree of controlled crying will have to be implemented if sleep-training is to be successful. With toddlers and babies who have already got into seriously bad sleeping habits, the following sleep-training techniques will need to be used along with the advice for sleeping and feeding requirements.

Controlled crying is always a last resort to sleep-training and is the most effective way to train babies over six months and toddlers. However, if these children are still feeding in the night, it is advisable to implement the core night method first so that you can be confident that your baby or toddler is not crying through genuine hunger. One of the main reasons that controlled crying fails for so many parents is that a vicious circle has arisen in which the baby or toddler continues to feed in the night and does not eat enough during the day, so he is genuinely hungry in the night. The core night method and diluting his milk feed in the night should see an increase in his appetite during the day. I would not recommend that a parent attempts controlled crying until they see an increase in the amount of food their child is eating during the day.

Dr Richard Ferber is widely recognised as America's leading authority in the field of children's sleep problems. His book *Solve Your Child's Sleep Problems* explains every aspect of children's sleep in great detail, as well as how problems evolve and how parents can resolve them. For older babies and children who are still feeding in the night, he advises gradually eliminating night feeds. If waking continues, he recommends controlled crying to break the habit. The controlled crying method is likely to be more successful if used at each of the baby's sleep-times. While this method does teach a baby or child how to get to sleep on his own, it can be difficult to endure and can fail because parents get very distressed listening to their baby or child cry for lengthy periods of time. They resort to picking up the baby after 30–40 minutes and rocking him to sleep, which usually creates an even worse sleep problem. The baby soon learns that if he cries long enough and hard enough, he will be picked up.

It can be very distressing to have to listen to your child crying for any length of time; however, if done properly, this method will improve even the worst sleeping problems within days. In my experience, with older babies and toddlers the problem is normally resolved within a week. For controlled crying to be successful it is essential that the baby or child learns to settle himself to sleep, no matter how long it takes.

The basic rules for controlled crying are as follows:

Day one

It is always best to start controlled crying in the evening on the first day. The same procedure should be carried out no matter how many times the baby or toddler wakes in the night. The following day it is important that you stick to the routine appropriate for your baby or toddler's age and that you use the same procedure when settling him for day-time naps as you use in the evening.

- Decide on a regular time to start the bedtime routine and stick to it. Allow at least one hour for the bath, milk feed and settling.

- Settle your baby or child in his bed before he gets too sleepy. Kiss him goodnight and leave the room.

- Allow a minimum of 5–10 minutes of crying before returning to reassure him. Reassurance should be kept to the minimum. You can stroke him or say 'ssh ssh', but he must not be picked up. Leave the room after two minutes even if he continues to cry.

- After the first half hour the time between visits should be increased by 5–10 minutes each time, to 15–20 minutes between visits.

- Continue with the checking plan every 15–20 minutes until the baby or toddler falls asleep. Reassurance should still be kept to a minimum of no more than two minutes and he must not be lifted out of the cot.

- If your baby wakes in the night, continue to follow the same plan as for the evening, gradually increasing the time between visits, until you are going in every 15–20 minutes.

Day two

- For the day-time naps it is important that you start where you left off in the night. Wait at least 20 minutes before checking your baby or toddler and continue to keep visits to his room to a maximum of two minutes, with the minimum of reassurance.

- If your baby or toddler does not fall asleep until nearer the time the routine states that he is meant to be getting up, allow him 15 minutes in the morning nap and 45 minutes at the lunchtime nap; this way he will not end up sleeping after 3pm in the day. If your baby is very tired he may need a short nap of 15 or 20 minutes late afternoon if he is to get through until bedtime without becoming over-tired.

- The second evening follow the same settling procedure as the first night, but this time wait 20–25 minutes before returning to the nursery. During visits on the second night you can reassure your baby by saying 'ssh ssh', but do not stroke or touch him.

- If your baby or toddler is still crying after the first hour, the time between visits should be increased to 35–40 minutes.

- If he wakes in the night, you should wait 45 minutes before checking him, and you should not speak to or stroke him. Reduce the time in the room to one minute.

Day three

- By the third day, the majority of babies and toddlers will be settling themselves at all sleep-times within 20 minutes and there is no need to check on them.

- If your baby backtracks at one of the sleep-times and you have to go back to checking him, start off with checking him every 15–20 minutes and increase the interval until you are back to 45–50 minutes.

- It is very important that by the third day a checking time of no less than 15–20 minutes is enforced. Do not go back to checking every 5–10 minutes, as this usually results in the baby or toddler getting more upset by your visits.

- Once your toddler has done a few days of settling within 20 minutes, you should be able to use the crying down method for getting him off to sleep at naps or in the evening. Within a couple of weeks the majority of babies and toddlers will be going to sleep without any fuss at all.

Gradual withdrawal
(18 months to 2½ years)

This method usually works best for toddlers between the ages of 18 months and two and a half years, particularly if they are sleeping in a bed and not a cot. It is generally seen as the most gentle approach to sleep-training, so if parents of younger children want to avoid using the controlled crying method, they could consider this approach. However, I have not found this method to be very effective with younger babies as it seems to upset them even more when their parents potter around the room or sit by the bed. If this method is to be successful, the parents have to have the patience to be consistent for several weeks and be aware that it will take a lot longer than using controlled crying.

Dr Olwen Wilson, a child psychologist at the Royal Sussex County Hospital, claims that a more gentle strategy she has devised will ease children into a good sleeping pattern within seven days, without stressing the child or the parents. She believes that children should be frequently supported while they are learning how to go to sleep without direct comfort from their parents.

Dr Wilson stresses the importance of establishing the same rituals every night: bath, bedtime story and settling the child in his cot or bed. However, unlike Ferber she advises the parent to stay in the room for a short spell once the child is settled in his bed, but to be unobtrusive. She suggests moving around the room or sorting a drawer out before leaving the room for a short spell. The parents must be prepared to leave and re-enter the room high times during the first few nights of the programme. The maximum number of times a parent might have to enter the room could be as high as 300. She believes that this process gets the child used to being alone without making him feel isolated and fearful. By the third night she says that the child will become settled enough to be left on his own for a period of five minutes or longer. On the fifth night the child may backtrack and want to go back to his old, familiar pattern of settling. If parents are persistent at this stage and do not give in, she says that by the end of the week the problem of settling will be hugely improved and, within a further week or two, the child will be happy to go off to sleep on his own.

This method takes a lot of determination and patience on behalf of the parents, as it can take hours every evening of going in and out of the room before they reach a period when the toddler is calm enough for the withdrawal method to progress. I think this method works if the mother has the energy to spend perhaps two or even three weeks working at the plan without any other distractions.

It can also take several weeks to see a marked improvement, and I believe that one of the reasons many parents find that it does not work is because they get exhausted by the procedure before the toddler does, and end up giving in and resorting to the old ways of getting the toddler to sleep. I will always attempt this method first, but in the majority of cases I find that we eventually have to resort to controlled crying.

Which approach?

To help decide which approach will work best for your baby or toddler, see the chart on page 37 advising on the amount of sleep required for your baby's age and the most common sleep problems experienced. This information will help you determine what is causing the excessive night-time waking.

3

The Young Baby – Birth to Six Months

Birth to Four weeks – what to expect

The amount of sleep a newborn baby needs varies considerably during the first few days. Some will sleep on and off between feeds, while others will spend much of the time between feeds fussing and fretting. On average most babies will need a total of around 16 hours' sleep a day during the first few weeks, although some can need up to 18 hours a day. Sleep at this stage is more like a series of short naps spread over a 24 hour period, and until your milk comes in it is too early to tell whether your baby is one that needs more sleep or less sleep, and whether his natural sleep cycle will determine a longer stretch of sleep at night from early on. In my experience, babies who had very active periods in the early evening or in the middle of the night while in the womb will more than likely (if allowed) continue with this sleep pattern after birth. A very sleepy baby, if allowed, can often go for three or four long spells of sleep without feeding, while others may be screaming for food every one to two hours. If your baby is one of the latter, you may experience a difficult few days until the your milk comes in, as you will obviously have to assume that every time he cries he is hungry.

During your stay in hospital you will be advised on your baby's feeding, and once you leave, you will be visited regularly by your health visitor. They will be monitoring your baby's progress and it is important that you follow their advice during these early days.

However, I would be very careful about allowing your baby to go longer than three hours without feeding in the early days. In my experience parents who take the term 'feeding on demand' too literally are much more likely to end up with feeding and sleeping problems. Some babies do not demand to feed and if allowed will often go up to five or six hours in between feeds. This results in the breasts not getting enough stimulation in those vital early days when the milk is coming in, and this is one of the main reasons women end up with a low milk supply.

Allowing your baby to feed little and often during the first 10 days will not only help establish a good milk supply but it will help you avoid the feeding all night syndrome. Start your day at 6 in the morning, and feed three-hourly between 6am and midnight. This should ensure that your baby only needs to wake once in the night for a feed. During the early days it is also important that you get lots of advice on the correct positioning for breastfeeding and how to latch your baby on well. Poor positioning will result in your baby not getting a full feed and not settling well, and can also lead to painful, cracked or bleeding nipples.

What to aim for

By the end of the first week, a baby who weighs over 7lb should manage to sleep for a stretch of four hours from the 10–11pm feed provided their feeding needs are being met during the day. Smaller babies may still need to feed three-hourly around the clock. In my experience all babies between two and four weeks of age who are healthy and well fed, and gaining 6–8oz each week, should manage to sleep for one longer spell of four to five hours. If you are following the contented little baby routines, this longer spell should happen in the night. If you ensure that your baby is properly awake while feeding, as well as for short spells after each feed during the day, he should settle well at nap-times and after a feed at 6pm and sleep until 10pm, at which time a good feed should ensure that he gets through to 2 or 3am.

At this stage the majority of babies will fall asleep on the breast while feeding, particularly at feeds just prior to sleep. Allowing your baby to fall asleep on the breast or in your arms and putting him in the cot while in a deep sleep can lead to the wrong sleep associations and excessive night-time wakings.

Always arouse your baby slightly so that he is aware he is going into his cot. Some babies may fuss or fret but it is important that they learn to settle themselves to sleep. Provided they have been well fed and winded and are ready to sleep, the majority will settle within five or ten minutes, although a few babies will fight sleep and may need 10–20 minutes to settle themselves. If your baby is not settling within 20 minutes it is important that you keep a detailed diary of your day to eliminate any possible causes.

By the end of the first month a typical day should look similar to the following:

7am	awake and feeding
8.30/9am	nap-time
10am	awake and feeding
11.30am	nap-time
2pm	awake and feeding
4–5pm	nap-time
5pm	awake and feeding
6pm	bath and bedtime routine
10/11pm	awake and feeding
2/3am	awake and feeding

The bedtime routine

Establishing a good bedtime routine and getting your baby to sleep well between 7pm and 10pm will also be a major factor in how quickly he will sleep through the night. A baby who feeds well at 6pm and settles to sleep well between 7pm and 10pm, will wake up refreshed and ready to take a full feed. The amount of milk he takes at this time will help determine how long he will sleep in the night. Between two and four weeks, he should manage to sleep through until between 2am and 3am, provided he takes the required amount of milk for his weight and has been awake properly for one hour.

Start the bedtime routine no later than 6pm. If your baby has not slept well at nap-times you may need to start earlier. Try to keep things very calm and quiet throughout the bath, and after the bath avoid lots of eye contact and talking, so that the baby does not become over-stimulated. Try always to do the last part of the feed in the room where the baby's bed is, keeping it dimly lit, so that you can quickly settle him in his cot before he falls asleep.

Twins

Establishing a routine from very early on is essential for parents of twins. Because twins are normally born slightly early, a pattern of feeding will more than likely have been established in the hospital. The majority of twins that I have helped care for were feeding three-hourly when they left the hospital. Because their birth weight was normally somewhere between 5 and 6lb, I continued to feed them three hourly until they weighed nearer 7lb. I would then continue to feed them three-hourly during the day but would let them sleep one longer spell of four hours in the middle of the night. Normally, somewhere between the third and fourth week, their weight had increased enough that I could let them go slightly longer than three hours at some of the day-time feeds as well as at night.

Establishing a routine with twins is very hard work but it is achievable. Although it normally takes longer to get them sleeping through the night, nearly all the sets I have cared for were sleeping through the night from their last feed at 10/11pm to 6/7am in the morning by 12 to 14 weeks.

The following guidelines should help you establish a routine from very early on and avoid the many long-term sleep problems often associated with twins.

- Do not allow your babies to go longer than three hours between feeds until they reach a weight of at least 7lb. It is of no benefit to let them sleep longer between feeds as their tummies are so small that they need to feed little and often to gain as much weight as possible in the early days. Once they have reached 7lb, their tummies will be able to hold more milk at a feed and then it is possible to let them go slightly longer.

- In my experience, staggering the feeds by 20 minutes means that you will, in the long-term, not end up with two babies screaming for food at the same time. This is very important once the mother is left on her own to look after both babies. Waking one baby at 6.45 am and offering most of the feed, means he should then be happy to sit in his chair for a short spell while you wake and give the second baby most of his feed. Once the second baby has had most of his feed he should be happy to sit in his chair while you change the first baby's nappy and offer him the remainder of the feed. You can then go back to the second baby and change his nappy before offering him the remainder of his feed.

- In the very early days it is easier if you can keep the babies on one level for most of the day. Trying to get them up and downstairs between feeds, particularly in the morning, can be very exhausting. I have found that having the sterilizer and all the equipment upstairs along with a small fridge was a lifesaver in the very early days. When possible, I would also try to fit a small futon or single bed into the nursery, so that the parents could take turns of sleeping in with the babies, allowing the one off-duty to get a good night's sleep in their own bedroom. Planning the nights so that each parent gets a stretch of sleep is very important. I used to get the mother to go to bed at 9pm and the father to do the feeds between 10pm and midnight. By the time the first twin woke in the night, normally around 1 or 2am, the mother had at least had three or four hours' sleep. Twins normally need more sleep during the first month than single babies but they also need more feeds. Sometimes only an hour can elapse between feeding one twin and the other one waking up. It is very important to accept whatever help you can get in the early days. Do not feel guilty about asking relatives and friends to help with shopping or household chores so that you can catch up on extra sleep during the day.

• I have always settled my twins in separate cots from the very beginning. I have found that they are much more likely to disturb each other when they are put to sleep in the same cot. I usually found that I had one twin who would start to fight sleep at around three weeks of age. When this happened I would, for several days, put him in a separate room and allow him to cry down without the risk of waking the other twin. However, I always had to go through a stage where they had to get used to each other's crying. This can be very difficult, because just as one got off to sleep the other one would start up. As long as I knew they were well fed and ready to sleep, I did not interfere with this settling process, because I had learned from experience that twins who were never allowed to get used to each other's crying would often continue to be difficult to settle in the evening and would go on waking up several times a night for most of their first year, and perhaps even longer.

• Keep clothing simple during the first month. All of my twins were kept in little white vests and white babygrows in the early days. It made washing so much easier when you could stick everything into the same load. If possible, invest in a tumble dryer: it is well worth the expense and means that you do not have to worry about ironing if you remove everything from the dryer the minute it is dry.

• If you are breast feeding, rent a heavy-duty electrical pump with a double pumping kit so that expressing takes less time. Double expressing also helps stimulate the milk supply, and if you express from the very early days you should be able to produce more than enough to feed both babies. Expressing milk earlier in the day also means that you can collect milk so that your partner can give the 10pm feed from a bottle.

• Do not feel guilty if you have to introduce some formula. It is better to do 80 per cent breast feeding than attempt to do 100 per cent but give up because of exhaustion after a couple of weeks. If you are giving formula, try to do it at the 10pm feed rather than topping up at every feed during the day. If breast feeding does not work, do not allow people to make you feel guilty. I know hundreds of sets of formula-fed twins who are growing up into very healthy happy adults.

Common problems

If your baby is not settling at nap-times or is waking up more in the night than the above routine suggests, it is advisable to keep a very detailed diary of your baby's feeding and sleeping pattern. It is also helpful to make notes of his behaviour during social time, how long it takes him to settle at nap-time and whether you have to assist him to sleep.

Listed below are the most common reasons why babies under one month are difficult to settle at nap-times or in the early evening:

• Hunger

• Day-time sleep

• Wind or colic

• Early morning waking

Hunger

If excessive night feeding and waking is to be avoided, the baby needs to have a minimum of six feeds between 7am and 11pm. To fit in this number of feeds, the day must start at 7am. It is also important that a baby gets enough to eat at each feed. In the early days most babies need a minimum of 25 minutes on the first breast, and a baby over 8lb in weight should be offered the second.

A formula fed baby needs 75–90ml (2½–3oz) of milk per pound of his body weight each day, divided into the number of feeds he is having. Breast-fed babies will be more likely to wake up several times a night if they do not get enough to eat at the 10pm feed and may need a top-up after this feed.

Case Study – Milly, aged four weeks

Problem: unsettled evenings

Cause: possibly colic, probably hunger

I was contacted by Milly's parents when she was nearly four weeks old. They had tried to follow the contented little baby routines from the very early days, but with little success. Milly would rarely settle for naps at the times the routines suggested and would cry and feed on and off all evening. She would eventually settle at 11pm, but only after her mother had topped her up with formula. Her parents were convinced that she was suffering from colic, as she would bring her legs up and scream as if in terrible pain when she cried. This would go on all evening, no matter how many times her mother put her to the breast.

When I enquired about her weight gain, her parents were unsure as they had not had her weighed for nearly two weeks, although she had regained her birth weight by the time she was two weeks old. I advised them to get her weighed and call me back once they had an accurate weight. They called back the following day to say that Milly had only put on 7oz in the last two weeks. This confirmed what I had suspected, that the reason Milly was so unsettled, particularly in the early evening, was hunger and not colic. When I took more details from her parents it also transpired that while they had followed the contented little baby routines to the letter where the sleeping and feeding were concerned, Laura, Milly's mother, had not expressed at the times suggested in the book. This meant that when Milly went through a growth spurt at three weeks she did not get the extra milk she required. The reason why it is so important to express during the early days of following the contented little baby routines is to ensure that the mother always produces more milk than the baby actually requires. This means that when a baby goes through a growth spurt, the mother can express slightly less at the first feed of the day, so ensuring that there is extra milk to satisfy the baby's increased needs.

As this did not happen with Milly, I advised her mother that she would have to top her up before the first two naps of the day to ensure that she got the extra milk she needed. The extra stimulation of emptying the breasts would help increase the milk supply and hopefully we would be able to get back to the original routine within a few days. I also suggested that Laura offer Milly a small top-up of formula after the bath, as I was sure that her milk supply was very low then.

Within a couple of days the screaming and fretfulness had stopped. However, Milly would still get upset when put in her cot. She would feed well and look sleepy but the minute she was put in the cot she would wake up screaming, only to fall asleep the minute she was picked up and held in either of her parents' arms. I explained that while we had resolved the feeding issue, Milly had probably also learned the wrong sleep associations having got used to being held for much of her sleep-time.

I suggested that they should try the crying down method to see if Milly would settle at nap-times and in the evening. Her parents were not totally convinced that the problem was a wrong sleep association and were sure that she was still suffering some sort of physical pain which prevented her from settling to sleep.

I was very concerned that the constant handling from one parent to the other was creating a long-term problem, but could understand that they did not want their very young baby to be left to cry.

I therefore suggested that if Milly had to be held during naps or in the evening, it should be done consistently and by only one parent. For the next three days I advised them not even to attempt to put Milly in her cot at nap-times or early evening. Instead one or the other should lie in a quiet, dark room with Milly and cuddle her throughout the whole of the sleep-time. It was important that the same person was with her during the allocated sleep-time and that she was not handed back and forth or walked around from room to room.

As I had predicted, Milly slept soundly in one or the other of her parents' arms at each allocated sleep-time.

After one week of this, her parents were also convinced that Milly was neither hungry nor in pain and were confident about trying the crying down method described on page 39.

The first evening Milly cried for 10 minutes before her parents checked her, then fell asleep after a further 10 minutes of intermittent crying. Her nap-times followed much the same pattern. Within a week the crying decreased and Milly was happy to settle in her cot, sleepy but awake.

During this time Laura had also been following my plan for increased milk supply, and within a further week Milly was having all of her feeds from the breast during the day, without a top-up. Her parents continued to give her a full formula feed at 10pm. On the occasions when Laura had had a hectic day and felt her milk supply might be low at 6.15pm, she would top Milly up with the milk she had expressed at 10pm the previous evening.

Day-time sleep

Sleeping too much during the day is another cause of excessive night-time waking. Even very small babies need to be awake for some of the time. If the baby is allowed to sleep for long spells between feeds during the day, he will more than likely start to wake up for longer in the night. Try to encourage your baby to stay awake for 1–1½ hours after day-time feeds. Between 7am and 7pm try to keep his day-time sleep to no more than five hours.

Wind – breast-fed babies

A breast-fed baby does not normally take in as much air as a bottle-fed baby and may not bring up wind after each feed. If your baby has not brought up his wind within a few minutes and seems happy, it is best not to spend ages trying to get the wind up, as the endless rubbing and patting on the back can actually cause more upset than the wind itself. A baby who is genuinely bothered by wind will scream and scream after a feed – nothing will console him until he manages to burp.

The following guidelines should be observed if your baby is showing signs of excessive wind:

- I have found that babies who are positioned incorrectly on the breast are more likely to be bothered with wind. Frequently I observe mothers holding their babies as if they were bottle feeding. This means the baby is not able to latch on to the breast properly, which results in him taking in more air than necessary. It is worthwhile arranging a home visit from your health visitor or your NCT breast feeding counsellor, who will teach you how to position your baby on the breast correctly.

- If you are confident that you are holding your baby properly and that he is positioned correctly on the breast, the wind may be caused by something you are eating. Occasionally babies react to certain foods that their mother has eaten. The pain usually occurs 12–16 hours after the mother has eaten the offending food. The main foods I have found to cause a reaction in babies, if eaten in excess, are dairy products, citrus foods, mushrooms and tomatoes. While tea, coffee, sugar and chocolate do not appear to cause wind, I do find that if taken in excess they can cause irritability in some babies. If you suspect a certain food may be causing your baby's wind, try cutting out that particular food for several days. If there is a marked improvement, wait a further week before introducing the food again, and even then do so gradually. However, if you find that the smallest amount of the suspect food causes your baby excessive wind, I would advise that you discuss this with your health visitor or doctor.

- It is essential that a breast feeding mother eat a varied and healthy diet and consume an extra 500 calories a day. Try to avoid too many convenience foods that are loaded with additives and empty starches. Also remember that this is not the time for dieting or excessive exercise; losing weight too quickly will not only reduce the amount of milk you produce, but could also result in the toxins that are accumulated in the fatty tissue being released into your breast milk. Some experts believe these toxins can cause irritability in some babies.

Wind – bottle-fed babies

While babies who are bottle-fed tend to take in more wind than breast-fed babies, this should not create a problem, as long as the baby is given the opportunity to burp once during the feed and once at the end. It is often assumed that burping a bottle-fed baby after every 30ml (1oz) will result in the baby taking in less wind. I have not normally found this to be the case, and more often than not I find that the baby gets distressed because the bottle is constantly being removed from his mouth. If your bottle-fed baby has problems bringing up his wind that leave him in a lot of discomfort, the first things that you should look at are the amount of formula your baby is taking and how often he is feeding. A formula-fed baby needs 75ml (2½oz) of formula per pound of his body weight each day. Refer to the chart on page 29 to determine whether you are feeding your baby the correct amounts. I believe that overfeeding is one of the major causes of excessive wind. Occasionally, a very hungry baby may need a little more milk a day, but if your baby is drinking 150ml (5oz) or more in excess of the recommended daily amount, then he could be overfeeding and this can cause severe wind pains.

The following guidelines may be of help if you find your baby is suffering from excessive wind.

- If you are sure that your baby is taking the right amount of formula for his weight, the next thing you should look at is the type of bottle you are using. I have found that the wide-necked bottle by Avent, with its specially designed teat, helps reduce the amount of air that a baby takes in.

- Pay extra attention when making up the formula feed: follow the manufacturer's instructions to the letter and make sure that you shake the bottle well, then shake it again to ensure that the water and formula are thoroughly mixed together.

- Before feeding your baby, loosen and re-screw the ring and teat back on to release any excess air.

- Ensure that you keep the bottle tilted so that the teat is filled with milk at all times. Keeping the baby in a more upright position during and after feeding also helps reduce the amount of air he takes in.

- Laying the baby flat on his back for a couple of minutes, then slowly raising him to a sitting position may help to release trapped air. Alternatively, lay the baby flat on his tummy with his head to one side, while gently rubbing his back.

- Some parents find that colic drops such as Infacol help their baby's excessive or trapped wind. There are also natural alternatives such as Chamomilla drops or Windypops, which contain camomile, fennel, catnip and lemon balm. Whether using conventional or alternative treatments, it is always advisable to discuss the correct dosages with a health visitor or qualified homeopath.

Colic

Excessive crying in babies under three months, is more often than not diagnosed as colic. The 'colicky baby' is usually described as being in great pain, screaming as he brings his knees up to his tummy, which is often distended and noisy. These long crying spells usually start in late afternoon or early evening and can last for several hours at a time. Opinion among healthcare experts is divided about what colic really is, and some do not believe it exists. Others believe that an immature digestive system and intestinal pain may be the causes of the crying and distended tummy.

Penelope Leach, author of several bestselling books on parenting and childcare, says in her book *Baby and Child* that colic is not an illness that needs diagnosis and treatment. She describes colic as a very distressing pattern of newborn behaviour with no known cause, no treatment and absolutely no ill effects except on the parents' nerves. She says that parents should accept that the cause of colic is unknown and there is very little they can do. She advises them not to search continually for the cause as this will only confuse other aspects of baby care by changing feeds, feeding techniques and routines, all to no avail. She suggests parents should instead concentrate on organising their life so that they have enough energy to give the baby the attention he needs during a 'colicky time'.

Dr Richard Ferber, in his book *Solve Your Child's Sleep Problem*, takes the view that a colicky baby is either oversensitive to things going on around him or is exposed to excessive amounts of handling and other stimulation. He believes that this 'chaotic' input is difficult for the baby to handle and may stem from a build-up of tension throughout the day to the point where his coping abilities become overloaded. Ferber disagrees with the majority of other experts' advice about how to deal with colic.

He says if the baby's needs were to be held, fed, rocked or given a dummy, these interventions would calm him. He advises that these babies should be given the opportunity to discharge tension at the end of the day. His guidelines are:

- If the baby cannot be easily comforted, allow him to cry alone for 15–30 minutes.

- If he has not settled by then, you may try to console him or feed him once again in a very calm, softly spoken and gentle manner.

- Parents should avoid trying to quieten the baby by bouncing or similar vigorous stimulation. If gentle attempts are not helpful, they should allow the baby to cry for another 15–30 minute period.

Ferber believes that allowing the baby to cry undisturbed for two or three colicky periods will give him the chance to release the built-up tension. He claims that the baby will then be better able to 'organise' himself and feel comfortable with daily routines. Within one or two days, he says, the intensity of crying should decrease and the baby should sleep better.

Dr Brian Symon believes that colic exists but he maintains it is a diagnosis that is overused and applied incorrectly. In his own practice it is his last choice as a diagnosis for excessive crying. In his book – *Silent Nights* – he says that for many parents colic simply means the baby is crying. He believes that the most common causes of babies crying are hunger and over-tiredness. His advice for dealing with colic is to ensure the baby is well fed, clean and dry, and firmly wrapped but not over-wrapped or hot. The treatment is then the same as for over-tired babies. Refer to page 40 for his crying down method.

The cure

Experts are divided as to what causes colic but the majority agree there is no magical cure. Both Leach and Dr Miriam Stoppard take the view that colic is something that parents have to learn to live with and that it normally disappears within three months. Sadly for parents struggling to cope with a colicky baby, what should be the happiest time of their lives can turn out to be one of the most miserable, with no amount of feeding, rocking, cuddling and walking stopping the hard and excessive crying.

As many parents of a colicky baby can confirm, the colic does disappear at three months but unfortunately the sleeping problems do not. All the rocking, cuddling, etc. involved in trying to calm the baby usually leads to the wrong sleep associations. He still refuses to settle in the evening and often wakes several times in the night. Each time he wakes he expects to be fed, rocked or cuddled back to sleep. This problem can continue for many months and often years.

I am often asked how I coped when my babies suffered from colic. The honest answer is that not one of the hundreds of babies I have helped care for has ever suffered from colic. I am convinced this is because I structured their feeding and sleeping from day one. If you follow a routine that ensures your baby is never allowed to be left hungry, over-tired or over-stimulated, then I am convinced that colic will not occur. This also means that the mother never becomes tense, which Stoppard believes can contribute to colic.

Since the publication of my first book, thousands of parents have contacted me for advice about how to deal with their colicky baby. My advice is always the same: follow a good routine that ensures the right feeding, sleeping and stimulation for your baby. For a guide to such a routine please see the age specific chapters in this book. For a detailed day-by-day routine, see *The New Contented Little Baby Book*. Those that do follow a routine tell me that their baby's colic usually disappears overnight!

I believe there are many different reasons for excessive evening crying or colic. If your baby is crying for hours every evening, it could be for one or more of the reasons listed below. By eliminating all these possible causes and following the routine appropriate for your baby's age, you should find that his excessive crying is greatly reduced.

- Many breast-fed babies are very unsettled in the evening because their mother's milk supply is low. I would strongly advise that you try topping up your baby with a bottle of either expressed or formula milk after the evening feeds. If things improve, it will be clear that a low milk supply is the problem. I would advise that you try to increase your milk supply by expressing to ensure that a low milk supply does not become a long-term problem which could cause you to give up breast feeding. Please refer to the section on page 68 for advice on expressing.

- Both breast-fed and bottle-fed babies should be fed no later than 2.15pm in the afternoon to ensure that that they take a really good feed at 5/6.15pm.

- Babies being fed on demand are more prone to colic. Gradually increase the times between feeds until your baby is feeding at the times recommended in the later sections of this book as appropriate for his age.

- Babies who are allowed to sleep late in the morning are unlikely to settle at 7pm. Regardless of how your baby has slept in the night, wake him at 7am. This will ensure that you can fit in the correct number of feeds before 7pm and that he has been awake enough time. Refer to page 16 for guidelines on the amount of day-time sleep your baby needs.

- A baby who is screaming at every feed and arching his back midway through a feed could be suffering from reflux and it would be worthwhile seeking medical advice.

Over-tiredness and over-stimulation

- Over-stimulation prior to bedtime can result in a baby becoming over-tired. Prior to the bath, start to wind things down – no loud noises or exciting games. Until the baby is settled in the routine, it is better if one person does the bath, feeding and settling. Constant handling from one person to another will only make a fretful baby worse.

- Over-tiredness is one of the main reasons that so many babies do not settle in the evening. Babies who are used to catnapping on and off during the day are more prone to over-tiredness.

Once you are confident that you are getting your baby's feeding and sleeping right, you may have to follow the advice for crying down on page 39. This advice will work provided your baby is getting enough milk to drink at the 6.15pm feed.

Expressing

I have always believed that expressing a small amount of milk during the early weeks of breast feeding can help avoid the problem of low milk supply. The enormous feedback from mothers who followed the routines in my first book is further evidence of this. Those mothers who followed my guidelines for expressing in the very early days, rarely experienced the problem of a low milk supply and very quickly established a regular feeding pattern. When their babies went through growth spurts every few weeks, the routine stayed intact, because any increased appetite could be immediately satisfied simply by expressing less milk at the early morning feeds. These babies continued to have a steady weight gain and gradually slept longer from the last feed, eventually going from 11pm–6/7am.

Unfortunately, the mothers who followed the routines but excluded the expressing were faced with a problem when their babies went through a growth spurt and needed extra milk. These mothers found they had to go back to feeding two- or three-hourly, and often twice in the night to increase their milk supply. This pattern of feeding was repeated each time their baby went through a growth spurt and made it very difficult to keep the routine going. Feeding two-hourly, more often than not, resulted in the baby being fed to sleep, and created a further problem of the wrong sleep association. Expressing is an excellent way of increasing a low milk supply and keeping the baby in a routine. If done from the very early days it can help to avoid altogether the problem of a low milk supply.

If you have previously experienced difficulties with expressing, do not be disheartened. Expressing at the times suggested in my routines, along with following the following guidelines, should help make it easier.

- The best time to express is in the morning, as the breasts are usually fuller. Expressing will also be easier if done at the beginning of a feed. Either express one breast just prior to feeding your baby, or feed your baby from one breast, then express from the second breast before offering him the remainder of his feed. Some mothers actually find that expressing is easier if done while they are feeding the baby on the other breast.

- In the early days, you will need to allow at least 15 minutes to express 60–90ml (2–3oz) at the morning feeds, and up to 30 minutes at the evening expressing times. Try to keep expressing times quiet and relaxed. The more you practise, the easier it will become. I usually find that by the end of the first month the majority of mothers can easily express 60–90ml (2–3oz) within five minutes at the morning feeds, and 180–240ml (6–8oz) within 10 minutes at the 10pm feed.

- An electric, heavy-duty expressing machine, the type used in hospitals, is by far the best way to express milk in the early days. The suction of these machines is designed to simulate a baby's sucking rhythm, encouraging the milk flow. If you are expressing both breasts at 10pm it is also worthwhile investing in an attachment that enables both breasts to be expressed at once, therefore reducing the time spent expressing.

- Sometimes the let down is slower in the evening when the breasts are producing less milk; a relaxing warm bath or shower will often help encourage the milk to flow more easily. Also gently massaging the breasts before and during expressing will also help.

- Some mothers find that it is helpful to have a picture of their baby close by for them to look at, while others find it better to watch a favourite television programme or to chat to their partner. Experiment with different approaches to see which one works best for you.

Early-morning waking

I believe that how parents deal with early-morning waking during the first few months will help determine whether their baby will become a child who is an early riser. In my experience all babies and children come into a light sleep between 5am and 6am. During the first few weeks, a baby who is waking and feeding between 2am and 2.30am may wake again between 5am and 6am and genuinely need to feed. Some will settle back to sleep for a further hour or so after this feed but many do not.

One of the main reasons that some babies do not settle back to sleep is that, because it is so near to morning, parents tend to treat the feed like a day-time feed and the baby becomes over-stimulated.

I have always treated any waking before 7am like a night-time waking. If the baby needed feeding I would do so quickly and quietly with the use of only a small socket night-light and without talking or eye contact. I would always settle the baby back to sleep until 7–7.30am, even if this meant they were only going back to sleep for 10–15 minutes. Whenever possible I would try to avoid changing the nappy as this usually wakes the baby up too much.

Once a baby is waking and feeding between 3am and 4am, waking at 6am is not usually related to hunger. This is the one and only time I would advise parents to help their baby return to sleep. At this stage the most important thing is to get him back to sleep quickly, even if it means cuddling him and offering him a dummy until 7am.

Listed below are the main causes of early-morning waking in babies up to the age of six months.

- Hunger should always be looked at as the first cause of a baby waking too early. With babies under two months, too small a feed in the middle of the night (i.e. the feed somewhere between 1am and 5am) is often the reason. Parents are often too eager to try to push their baby through the night and assume that giving the baby a smaller feed in the middle of the night will be the quickest way to eliminate that feed. The middle of the night feed should never be reduced until the baby has shown that he can sleep happily to 7am for at least one week. Then it can gradually be reduced every few nights by a small amount provided he is sleeping through to 7am and continues to gain weight. With babies between two and four months who are sleeping through most of the night, too small a feed at 10pm is often the cause of early waking and the baby should be offered more at that feed. Breast-fed babies may need to be offered a top-up of expressed or formula milk from a bottle if they are emptying both breasts.

- When the baby is over four months parents, often drop the 10pm feed before he is taking enough solids. Ensure that your baby is well established on solids for at least two weeks and only taking a very small feed before dropping it. Once he drops the 10pm feed he may also start to wake up early because he is not getting enough to eat at the 7pm feed. Formula-fed babies may need an extra 30ml (1oz) or so at that feed. With breast fed babies it may be necessary to top-up with either breast milk or formula milk if the baby is emptying both breasts.

- During the first two to three months it is important to have the baby fully awake at the 10pm feed for at least an hour. Once the baby is sleeping through regularly to 7am for at least a week, you can gradually cut back on the time he is awake at 10pm. Reducing it by 10 minutes every three nights provided he continues to sleep through to 7am, will ensure that he does not end up waking earlier. Once the baby is over four months old, is taking only a small feed at 10pm, is awake for only 20 minutes and solids are well established, this waking time can be dropped. Once the 10pm feed has been dropped it is important to try to encourage your baby to stay awake until 7pm.

- Next to hunger, light filtering around the side of curtains or above a curtain pole is a major cause of early waking. Research shows that the chemicals in the brain work differently in the dark, preparing it for sleep. In my experience even the smallest chink of light can be enough to waken a baby fully when he comes into a light sleep between 5am and 6am. Large gaps that allow light to stream under the door can also create a problem, as can leaving the door slightly open or a small night-light on.

- Kicking off the bedcovers can also cause babies under six months to wake early. In my experience all babies under this age sleep better when tucked in securely. The sheet needs to be placed lengthways across the width of the cot to ensure that a minimum of 20cms (8in) is tucked in at the far side and a minimum of 10cm (4in) tucked in at the near side. I would also advise rolling up a small hand towel and pushing it down between the spars and the mattress at the near side. Babies who work their way up the cot and get out of the covers will benefit from being put in a lightweight, 100 per cent cotton sleeping bag and tucked in with a sheet as described above. Depending on the weather, blankets may be necessary.

Case Study – Sophia, aged four weeks

Problem: early-morning waking

Cause: sleepy 10pm feed

Sophia weighed nearly 10lb at birth and went straight into the two-to-four week routine. She fed well and slept well at the right times. When she reached four weeks she started sleeping through till 6.30–7.30am from the 10pm feed. She had done this consistently for two weeks but her parents did notice that she was waking earlier and earlier every morning. By the time she was six weeks she was waking at 5am and not interested in feeding but would not go back to sleep until nearly 6.30am.

Her mother would then let her sleep until 7.30am, when she would get her up and feed her. She would then follow the routine to the letter throughout the whole day. Sophia was feeding well at each feed and gaining 8oz each week. Baffled by why she should suddenly backtrack on her night-time sleep, I decided to spend the day with the family. Throughout the whole day I saw no obvious reason for Sophia's early waking. She fed well and was awake for the right amount of time after feeds.

However, at the 10pm feed she drank her milk very quickly and by 10.20pm there was only 30ml (1oz) of the feed left. Sophia then got very sleepy and even the nappy change did not wake her. She took the last 30ml (1oz) in a very drowsy state was back in bed by 10.35pm.

I came to the conclusion that this very quick and rather sleepy feed was the cause of Sophia's early morning waking. Until a baby is between three and four months old, he will need to wake up properly somewhere between 7pm and 7am. Because Sophia had dropped her middle of the night feed at a young age and was very sleepy at the 10pm feed, her waking time had moved to 5am.

I suggested to her parents that for the following week they should wake Sophia as normal at 10pm but not feed her until 10.20pm. This would ensure that she was properly awake before she began feeding. They should then give her two-thirds of the feed before her nappy change. Then, instead of giving her the remainder straight away, they should wait 15–20 minutes. During this time she could be laid on their bed for a stretch and a kick to make sure she stayed properly awake. But they were to avoid lots of talk and eye contact as this could confuse her, making her think it was day-time. After 20 minutes they should dim the lights and offer her the remainder of her feed and settle her back in bed by 11.30pm. Within three nights Sophia was back to sleeping right through to 7am.

I advised the parents to continue with this longer waking at 10pm for a further week and then gradually reduce the length of time she was awake by 10 minutes. Provided she continued to sleep through to 7am, they should continue reducing the time awake by 10 minutes every three days. By the time she reached 10 weeks, Sophia was able to sleep through to 7am with only a 30-minute waking at the 10pm feed.

One to four months – what to expect

By the time a baby has reached one month, a more predictable pattern of feeding and sleeping should have emerged. He will be showing signs of being much more alert during awake times and managing to stay awake longer. Babies who have managed to stay awake for an hour will normally extend it to nearer one and a half hours at this stage. Babies who have managed to stay awake for one and a half hours will usually manage to stay awake for nearer two hours. The majority of babies will cut back slightly on their day-time sleep, and naps during the day should become more predictable, with a couple of short naps and one longer one. The baby is capable of taking bigger feeds and therefore of going longer in between feeds. He is also capable of going slightly longer during a 24-hour day. If you have been structuring his day-time feeding and sleeping, this should happen from the late evening feed. If you are still feeding your baby on demand, it is advisable to begin to implement a routine now, if you wish to avoid your baby cutting down or cutting out altogether a feed at the wrong time of the day.

By the time they reach four months the majority of babies are capable of sleeping right through the night from 10/11pm until 6/7am. While many babies will fall into a routine naturally, a

Listed below are the main causes of unsettled evenings and excessive night-time waking of healthy babies between one and four months of age.

Common problems

If your baby is not feeding or sleeping at similar times to those suggested on page 76 and is not settling at nap-times or is waking excessively in the night, I would advise that you start him off on a routine similar to that for a one-month-old (see on page 53). Once you have managed to get him feeding and sleeping at those recommended times you can very quickly progress towards the routine suitable for his age by decreasing each of his daytime naps by a few minutes each day until he is happily sleeping and staying awake at the recommended times. If you find that he is having problems adapting to the routines, one or more of the following problems may be the cause:

- Hunger (see page 57)
- Wind and Colic (see pages 61–7)
- Early-morning waking
- Day-time sleep
- Dummy dependence (wrong sleep association)
- Night-time waking and solids

Early-morning waking

At this stage many babies under eight weeks may be sleeping through from the last feed until 5am or 6am and wake up and genuinely need to feed. This is not a problem provided the feed is treated like a night-time feed and the baby settles back to sleep fairly quickly. If your baby is over eight weeks of age and waking at 5am or 6am it may be that he is not feeding well at the last feed, and it would be worthwhile trying to increase this feed to see if this will help him to sleep right through the night. For some babies the early-morning waking may be caused by other reasons than hunger.

The most common ones are early-morning light or the baby kicking off the bedcovers.

Case Study – Joseph, aged ten weeks

Problem: early-morning waking

Cause: light in the bedroom and a strong Moro reflex

Joseph was a fourth baby and, like his brother and two sisters, went straight into the routine. Like Sophia he would wake early, refuse to feed and want to stay awake for over an hour. His brother and sisters had all slept through the night by the time they were eight weeks, so his mother knew the importance of having him properly awake at the 10pm feed and taking a good feed. It therefore came as a bit of a shock to his mother when he reached 10 weeks and was still waking at 5am.

She would always give him the benefit of the doubt, assuming that he might be hungry and offering him the breast. He would suck for a couple of minutes, then begin to scream hysterically and arch his back, refusing to feed. She would end up rocking and cuddling him for over an hour to get him back to sleep. He would awake happy at around 7am, take a full breast feed and follow the routine to the letter for the rest of the day. His mother could not fathom what was causing these early-morning wakings. His day-time sleep was perfect. He fed well and his room had both a black-out blind and curtains lined with black-out material.

Obviously, with three other children to take care of, starting the day at 5am began to take its toll on Joseph's mother. When she rang me for advice I could think of no obvious reason for the early-morning waking. I suggested that she sleep in Joseph's room for a couple of nights to monitor his sleeping pattern.

That night she fed him his one formula feed of the day at 10.30pm and kept him wide awake for an hour before tucking him very securely in his cot. She checked that the curtains were properly drawn and the door securely closed before settling herself down to sleep. At different intervals throughout the night he came into a light sleep, moving his body for a few minutes, sometimes groaning a little before going back to sleep. Then at 4.45am a bright stream of light suddenly appeared under the door. Joseph immediately began to stir. He tossed his head from side to side and within 10 minutes was wide awake and had pushed himself to the top of the cot. His head then turned in the direction of the stream of light under the door and he began to thrash his arms and legs up and down in the air and cry hysterically.

The cause of the problem was obvious. Slight subsidence in the family's very old house created a gap of nearly 2cm (1in) under the bedroom door. Sudden light appeared when Joseph's father left for work and didn't close the inner hallway door. The light was strong enough to arouse Joseph from his light sleep. He also still had a very strong Moro reflex, which caused him to get very upset after he had worked his way loose from the bedcovers.

I advised the parents to fit a draft excluder to the bottom of the door to ensure that no light could stream in under it and to put Joseph in the lowest tog lightweight sleeping bag at night.

The sleeping bag, along with tucking in the sheet well around the cot would prevent him moving up the cot. I advised that if Joseph continued to wake at 5am, then his mother should not rush to him when he stirred. The first three days he grizzled on and off for 30–40 minutes, then settled back to sleep until 7am. From then on Joseph slept through until 7am.

Day-time sleep

What happens during the day continues to play a big part in how well a baby sleeps at night. A baby who is allowed to sleep too much during the day may wake up too much in the night. Likewise, a baby who sleeps too little may also wake up in the night, usually because he has learned the wrong sleep associations during the day-time sleep.

Case Study – Harriet, aged 12 weeks

Problem: sudden night-time waking after sleeping through

Cause: cutting back on the lunchtime nap

Harriet weighed over 9lb at birth and happily went straight into the two-to-four week routine. She followed the routines like clockwork during the day and regularly slept through the night from three weeks of age.

Things had started to go wrong when she was around three months, which coincided with the time a nanny was employed. The nanny began to lengthen the time of Harriet's morning and to cut back on her lunchtime nap so that they could attend various play dates in the afternoon. The shorter lunchtime nap meant that Harriet started to get tired and irritable in the late afternoon. The bath and bedtime routine quickly went from being a happy and relaxing event to a very tearful one.

Harriet's parents insisted that her naps were changed back to the original times. Unfortunately, even though the morning nap was cut back to 40 minutes, Harriet would fully awaken from her light sleep during the lunchtime nap and not resettle. They tried feeding her, giving her the dummy – nothing worked. Eventually, they tried leaving her to cry, but she got so distressed that they ended up picking her up after 20 minutes. This went on for a couple of

weeks and the parents had more or less resigned themselves to the fact that they had lost the long lunchtime
sleep. Then, to their horror, Harriet (now 4 months old)
started to wake up several times at night. Every time she
came into a light sleep, she would cry out until one of her
parents went in and helped her to settle back to sleep. That
was when they decided to call me for help.

I explained that in order to get Harriet back to sleeping
well at night, we would have to sort out her day-time sleep.
I believed that it was essential for Harriet to learn to settle
herself back to sleep when she surfaced from light sleep 45
minutes into her lunchtime nap.

On the first day of sleep-training, when Harriet came
into her light sleep, I advised the parents to wait 10–15
minutes before checking her. They could then go in for two
minutes, stroke her forehead and say 'ssh ssh' but under
no circumstances were they to pick her up. She cried on
and off for the remaining hour of her lunchtime nap. She
woke twice in the night for 40–45 minutes each time and
the parents used the same approach as during the day.

The following day I advised them to wait 20–25 minutes
before going in to her at her lunchtime nap and the same
at night-time. She cried for much the same time during the
lunchtime sleep as the previous day but woke only once
in the night, crying on and off for 50 minutes.

On the third day I told the parents that they should try
to resist going in at all during the lunchtime nap. Her pattern was much the same as the previous two days.
However, in the night she only had one very brief waking
and settled herself back to sleep within 15 minutes.

On the fourth day during her lunchtime nap Harriet woke
after 45 minutes and settled back to sleep within 15 minutes. She then woke again briefly after a further 45 minutes
and settled herself back to sleep within five minutes. That
night her parents heard her moaning and groaning when

she came into her light sleep at 3am and again at 4.30am but she did not cry out.

For a further week during her lunchtime nap she would cry out when she came into her light sleep but for shorter and shorter times. She continued to sleep well at night and by the end of two weeks she was back to her old routine of sleeping well at lunchtime, as well as at night. The crying and irritability in the late afternoon disappeared, as she was no longer tired from lack of sleep.

Harriet is now nearly two years old and continues to sleep well from 7pm to 7.30am, with a two-hour nap in the middle of the day.

Dummy dependence

A dummy can be a great comfort to some babies in the early days, particularly a sucky or sensitive baby. I have used dummies with the majority of my babies and it never created a problem because I never allowed the baby to fall asleep with the dummy in his cot. A baby who has become used to falling asleep with the dummy in the evening, will more than likely begin to wake up at least two or three times more in the night and need it to get back to sleep. This is not a problem that resolves itself and is better dealt with sooner than later. Some babies can end up waking up every hour looking for the dummy, and, if not dealt with, this can go on for two and some-times three years. Unfortunately, it is not a problem that can be resolved without some degree of crying, but, fortunately, unlike some other problems, it is usually resolved within a few nights.

Case Study – Harry, aged 15 weeks

Problem: difficult to settle to sleep and waking up several times a night

Cause: sleep association caused by dummy dependence

Harry had been a very sucky baby since birth and would spend hours feeding on the breast. It would take ages to settle him to sleep and he would only do so if allowed to suck himself to sleep on the breast.

By the time he was eight weeks old, he was waking every couple of hours in the night and would only settle back to sleep when sucking on the breast – only to wake up one or two hours later.

Harry's parents assumed that his constant need for the breast was hunger, and they decided to switch to bottle feeding, so they could feel confident he was getting enough to eat. Harry took to bottle feeding very easily and would drink the right amount for his weight but was still very difficult to settle. It was then that Harry's mother, Lucinda, on the advice of a friend, introduced a dummy to try to get Harry to sleep. For several weeks the dummy seemed a godsend.

Lucinda and her partner could put Harry in his cot with the dummy and he would suck himself to sleep. When he stirred a couple of hours later, provided they got to him quickly enough and stuck the dummy back in, he would go straight back to sleep. Although they were getting up two or three times a night to put the dummy back in, it was not as exhausting for Lucinda as having him attached to her breast for hours at a time. However, as the weeks went by and Harry became more active, the dummy would drop out more and more as he moved about in his sleep. By the time Harry reached 15 weeks, his parents were having to go in every 45 minutes to an hour to put the dummy in his mouth.

They were at their wits' end with sleep deprivation, and with Lucinda about to return to work in a couple of weeks they knew that they would never cope if they could not crack the problem of Harry's extreme need for the dummy.

They decided to try allowing Harry to have the dummy to fall asleep but removing it the minute he was asleep. Sometimes this worked – and sometimes it did not. Harry's day-time sleep now also started to be seriously affected by his need for the dummy and, in addition, he started to get irritable and agitated looking for the dummy throughout his awake time.

It was at this point that his parents telephoned me for advice. They realised that there was going to be no gentle way of getting rid of the dummy, but, like most parents, they were concerned about the length of time they should leave Harry to cry. I agreed that in my experience cold turkey was the only way to eliminate dependency on the dummy quickly.

I explained to Lucinda how controlled crying worked (see page 45) and told her that, provided they followed the guidelines properly, Harry should get over his dummy addiction within three nights. However, I emphasised how important it was that both she and her husband were in agreement about going down the controlled crying route, as when not carried out consistently – for example when a baby is left to cry for a long period and then picked up and cuddled by a parent who cannot cope with the crying – it can make matters worse.

Lucinda and her husband both agreed to start the training procedure that night. As instructed, they settled Harry in his cot sleepy but awake and without the dummy, and left the room. Harry started to scream immediately. They both agreed to wait 10 minutes before one of them entered the room. Lucinda then went and stroked his tummy for a couple of minutes, then quickly left the room. She knew it was important not to talk to him or take him out of the cot. She repeated this procedure during the next 45 minutes, by which time Harry had fallen asleep. He woke up twice in the night and his parents carried out the same procedure as earlier. The first time he settled within 30 minutes and on the second waking within only 10 minutes.

Because it was important not to confuse Harry, it was

essential that he not be given his dummy at day-time naps. However, I did not want him to get over-tired, so the following day Lucinda took Harry for a long walk in his buggy at each of his day-time naps. She knew that the motion of the buggy would make him less fretful and less likely to scream for the dummy.

The next night his parents used the same procedure for settling him, only they waited 15 minutes before going in. They were just about to go in for the second time when Harry stopped crying and went to sleep. That night he only woke once in the night and settled back to sleep within 20 minutes. The following day Lucinda took him out in the buggy again at naptimes to ensure that he slept without the dummy and didn't get over-tired.

On the third night Harry settled within 20 minutes and Lucinda did not need to go in at all – he slept right through the night. The next day we agreed that Harry should be put in his cot for day-time naps. Both times he settled within 10–15 minutes.

Harry very quickly found his thumb and within a week was happy to settle in his cot without any crying. His parents would often hear him stir when he came into his light sleep in the night, but he rarely cried out and more often than not would use his thumb to settle himself to sleep.

Night-time waking and solids

The recommended age for introducing solids is between four and six months. Weaning before this age to encourage babies to sleep better rarely works and can have disastrous and even dangerous consequences. It can also increase the risk of a baby developing allergies and can damage his digestive system. Do not be pressurised into weaning early just get your baby sleeping through the night. In my experience, many parents think their baby is ready to be weaned because he is waking two or three times a night and wanting to feed.

In fact the reason the majority of babies over eight weeks are waking in the night hungry is not because they are ready for solids but because they are not getting full milk feeds during the day.

A full milk feed is either a formula feed of 240ml (8oz) or a feed from both breasts. If your baby is under four months and feeding more than once in the middle of the night, it is highly unlikely that he is taking five full feeds between 7am and 11pm. If this is the case, it would be advisable to use the core night method to reduce his night-time wakings and feedings. This should help improve his day-time feeding, which should in turn reduce his night-time wakings and feedings.

A baby is ready to be weaned when he shows signs that his appetite is no longer satisfied by four to five milk feeds a day. This rarely happens before four months. However, if your baby is taking five full milk feeds a day, it is much better to keep feeding in the night for a few more weeks than put your baby's health at risk by offering solids too early.

Case Study – Antonia, aged 12 weeks

Problem: waking several times a night, sometimes screaming for long stretches

Cause: formula milk and solids

Antonia was born three weeks early and weighed in at 6lb 2oz. Her mother Lucy was determined to give her the best possible start in life and breast feed her on demand for the first six weeks. Unfortunately, Antonia's weight gain was very poor – only 2–3oz a week. She was feeding every couple of hours around the clock, and by six weeks Lucy was so exhausted with the lack of sleep and trying to care for a new baby and a very demanding toddler that she started to supplement each breast feed with formula. Unfortunately, the top-up formula feeds caused Lucy's milk supply to decrease even further and by the time Antonia reached eight weeks she was being totally formula-fed.

This did not seem to solve the problem of Antonia wanting to feed little and often. In desperation Lucy switched her on to the second stage milk for hungrier babies. Two weeks later things had got worse, with Antonia rarely sleeping more than a couple of hours at a time and often screaming for up to four hours. When Antonia reached 10 weeks of age, Lucy sought expert help and was advised to start giving her solids. By the time Antonia was 12 weeks old, she was on three solid meals a day plus six to eight small milk feeds. But the hours of screaming and the sleepless nights continued. Lucy was told she must accept that some babies do scream a lot in the first few months and that Antonia was obviously going to be one of those babies. It was at this stage that she telephoned me for help.

While it was not clear what was causing the problem, I shared Lucy's view that it is not natural or normal for a young baby to cry for hours the way Antonia did. The first thing I advised her to do was gradually change Antonia back to the first stage formula milk. Second stage milk is much heavier than first stage milk and takes longer to digest. I explained to Lucy that a hungry baby is one who is drinking a 240ml (8oz) bottle of formula and showing signs of hunger after a couple of hours. This was clearly not the case with Antonia, as she never took more than 120ml (4oz) at a feed. I was also very unhappy about her being given solids, as the current advice is not to introduce solids before the age of four months. Lucy was happy to change milk and cease giving solids to Antonia.

By the second day of the new regime Antonia was settling at 7pm, sleeping a good six hours, taking a feed of 120–130ml (4–5oz) and then settling back to sleep without any fuss for a further six to seven hours. The screaming had stopped. The transformation in 24 hours was amazing. I am firmly convinced that the combination of the heavier milk and solids was too much for Antonia's digestive system to cope with and was the cause of the hours of screaming and sleepless nights.

Four to six months – what to expect

The majority of babies are capable of sleeping right through the night from the last feed by the time they reach four months, although a totally breast-fed baby may still need a feed between 5am and 6am if they are not getting enough to drink at the 10/11pm feed. Between four and six months is the recommended time for solids to be introduced, and once they have been established twice a day, the baby should start to cut back on the late feed, eventually sleeping 11–12 hours a night.

What to aim for

Once solids are introduced it is very important that any milk feeding after 7pm and before 7am in the morning is greatly reduced, and eliminated altogether before the baby reaches six months.

Even babies who have been going a longer spell in the night can suddenly start to wake up several times a night if milk feeding and solid feeding is not structured properly. If your baby is still waking up in the middle of the night looking for a night feed once solids are introduced, it would be advisable to implement the 'core night' method to reduce these feeds. It is also very important to ensure that solids are introduced at the right times to ensure that the baby does not cut down too quickly on the amount of milk he is drinking. In *The Contented Little Baby Book of Weaning* I give a guide to what to introduce and when between four and six months of age. If you are unsure as to whether your baby is getting the right balance, check the guidelines in this book.

The bedtime routine

By six months the bedtime routine has changed and a baby will be having some solids at 5pm, with only a small drink of milk or water from a beaker. His full milk feed will come after the bath, usually around 6.30pm, although some babies can stay awake slightly later and could have their milk feed nearer 7pm. Some parents introduce a bedtime story at this age. The story consists of looking at very simple picture books and repeating simple phrases to describe the picture. It is important that this should be kept to a maximum of 10 minutes; any longer than this can over-stimulate young babies.

The majority of babies who have slept well during the day will go down in their cot and often babble to themselves for 10 or 20 minutes before falling asleep.

A baby who does not sleep well during the day often becomes very over-tired and goes straight into a deep sleep the minute he goes in the cot. This can have the knock-on effect of him waking much earlier in the morning, and a vicious circle soon sets in of him going to sleep earlier for his first nap because he woke up so early. If your baby is getting very tired by 6.30pm, it is important to look at his day-time sleep to ensure that a long-term problem of going to sleep too quickly is not established.

Common problems

- Hunger
- Early-morning waking
- Illness

Case Study – Tara, aged five months

Problem: waking in the middle of the night hungry

Cause: introducing the wrong types of solids at the wrong time

Tara was breast-fed on demand for the first seven weeks of her life. It was nearly four weeks before she regained her birth weight, and at six weeks her weekly weight gain was so low that her mother was advised to top up after each breast feed with formula milk. By seven weeks she was getting virtually all her feeds from the bottle. Her mother had breast-fed her other two children for three months, and she was keen to do the same for Tara. She contacted me for advice. I suggested that she follow my plan for a low milk supply (see page 68) for one week.

Because Tara's mother's milk supply was so low, I advised that she should top up with formula milk instead of expressed milk after the 10.30am feed, as the plan suggests. Within one week her milk supply had increased so much that Tara was taking the breast at all her day-time feeds, with a top-up of expressed milk after the 10.30am and 6.15pm feeds. She continued to have one formula feed at 11pm and by the end of the eighth week was happily in the six-to-eight-week routine, and sleeping through to 7am from her last feed. Tara continued to feed well from the breast and gained 8oz in weight each week until she was three months old. At this stage her mother gradually began to introduce more formula milk, and by four months Tara was on four full milk feeds a day and sleeping 7pm to 7am, and had started solids.

Things continued to go well for a further six weeks until one night Tara suddenly woke up at 2am. Her mother was concerned that she might genuinely be hungry as she had only taken 150ml (5oz) at the 6pm feed, so she offered her a small 120ml (4oz) feed. Tara drank this quickly but still refused to settle back to sleep until she was given a further 120ml (4oz) of formula. She then went to sleep quickly and had to be woken at 7am.

During the following week Tara became more and more difficult over her day-time milk feeds. A pattern soon emerged in which she would take only 120–150ml (4–5oz) at each of her day-time feeds and often only 90ml (3oz) at

6.15pm, before waking up desperately hungry between 2am and 3am.

When her mother contacted me for further advice, she assured me she was still following my routines and guidelines to the letter. The daily records she sent me showed that the timing of the milk feeds and solids was correct. However, she had decided to introduce certain foods that are more difficult to digest earlier than I recommended. Banana, which I advise introducing at six months, was added to Tara's breakfast cereal at five months. Tara loved banana, and this prompted her mother to offer it to her regularly at lunchtime, along with mashed avocado, another food that is hard to digest.

Tara had been allowed to take the lead with weaning, which meant she cut back too quickly on her daily milk intake. As a result she was having to wake in the night to make up for the milk she was no longer getting during the day. It was clear from her feeding charts that Tara, who then weighed 15lb, had cut back too dramatically on her milk intake during the day because her solids had been increased too rapidly (especially at breakfast). This in turn affected the amount of milk she was taking at lunchtime. I advised her mother to cut back the breakfast cereal to two teaspoonfuls, with one or two cubes of pear or peach purée, instead of five teaspoonfuls of breakfast cereal with mashed banana.

Lunch, which also consisted of hard-to-digest fruits such as banana and avocado, was replaced by four to six cubes of vegetable purée, made up of a combination of potato and a choice of other vegetables.

After the 6pm feed I suggested that Tara be given four to six teaspoonfuls of baby rice mixed with two cubes of fruit instead of vegetable purée.

Within three days, Tara was back to sleeping from 7pm to 7am. The problem of milk underfeeding was caused by introducing too much of the wrong types of food too early or at the wrong time. This is a very common mistake, and is the main reason for babies under six months cutting back too quickly on their day-time milk, which results in a genuine need for a milk feed in the night.

Case Study – Edward, aged five months

Problem: early-morning waking

Cause: dropping 10pm feed too early and introducing solids at the wrong time

Edward was one of those easy babies who slipped into a good routine from the very early days. By the time he was eight weeks old he was settling well at 7pm and having to be woken at his parents' bedtime for his last feed. He would then sleep through to 6.30/7am every morning. At around 10 weeks he started to lose interest in his late night feed, sometimes taking as little as 60ml (2oz). His parents felt confident that Edward did not need a late night feed and at 11 weeks decided to drop it altogether. For a couple of weeks Edward continued to sleep from 7pm in the evening through until 6.30/7am, feeding four-hourly throughout the day. Then one morning his parents were suddenly awoken at 6am by Edward crying. They went to him immediately and tried to comfort and settle him back to sleep with a cuddle. Forty minutes later he was still fretful and unsettled and, although they were not convinced that it was hunger, they decided to feed him. He drank a 210ml (7oz) bottle in less than 10 minutes and promptly went back to sleep. Over the next couple of weeks Edward began to wake earlier and earlier and would not settle unless he was given a feed.

His parents realised that the cause of Edward's early waking was genuine hunger and decided to go with this pattern, as he would feed very quickly and settle straight back to sleep. They felt that it was pointless to reintroduce the late night feed as Edward could be weaned in three weeks time and they felt the introduction of solids would resolve the problem.

At 16 weeks Edward was taking a 210ml (7oz) bottle at 5am in the morning and settling back to sleep until 7am, when he would awake and take a further 120ml (4oz) of milk. Because he was not taking a full feed at 7am he started to look for another milk feed around 10am. His parents decided it would be a good idea to introduce him to solids after the 10am feed so that he would get through to 2pm for his next feed. However, much to their disappointment, the introduction of solids did not resolve the problem of Edward's early morning hunger. He continued to wake up and look for food around 5am every morning. Ten days later they decided to introduce solids at 5pm in the hope that solids later in the day would help Edward sleep longer. This had an immediate effect and Edward started to sleep until nearer 6am. All went well for a couple of weeks and as they gradually increased the baby rice in the evening Edward started to sleep later and later in the morning.

Then one evening Edward suddenly refused to drink his milk at 6.30pm. His parents struggled for an hour to get him to take 120ml (4oz). Concerned that he would wake early because he had not drunk enough, they decided to wake him at 10pm to see if they could get him to take a further 120ml (4oz). Their attempts were in vain, as Edward was in such a deep sleep that he could not be roused. As they anticipated, he awoke at 5am screaming for food. It was at this stage that they contacted me.

I explained that the problem they were experiencing was a very common one amongst parents who allow their baby to drop the 10pm feed too early.

Even if a baby is taking only 60ml (2oz) at 10pm, I advise parents to continue to wake him and offer him a feed until he is past four months and solids are established, the reason being that all babies will go through a growth spurt between three and four months and four milk feeds a day will rarely meet their hunger needs. If they have been allowed to drop the late feed, they will obviously have to wake up to satisfy their hunger. When this happens, most parents will try to re-introduce the 10pm feed to get the baby going longer in the night again. Unfortunately, this doesn't always work if the baby has got used to being in a deep sleep at this time.

While the introduction of solids at 5pm resolved Edward's problem in the short term, the rapid increase of solids led to a sudden decrease in the amount he was taking from his last bottle, and that is why his parents ended up with early-morning wakings a second time. Until a baby is well past six months it is important that he has most of his milk before the solids. This ensures that he will take exactly the amount of solids he needs to satisfy his hunger. Milk is still very important at this stage and he still needs a full milk feed of 210–240ml (7–8oz) or a breast feed from both breasts to get through the night. Giving the baby the solids first often leads to a baby increasing the amount he takes too rapidly and reducing the amount of milk too quickly.

I gave Edward's parents two options: bringing his bath forward to 5.45pm and giving him 180ml (6oz) of his milk after the bath, followed by his baby rice, followed by a further 60ml (2oz) of milk; alternatively, if he was too hungry to wait until after the bath, giving him 180ml (6oz) of milk at 5.30/6pm followed by his baby rice, delaying the bath until 6.30pm and offering him a further 60ml (2oz) of milk after the bath. They found that the second option worked better for them, as Edward got very fretful by

5.30pm. Because Edward had got into the habit of waking up early, he continued to do so for a couple of days, but his parents managed to settle him back with a few sips of cool boiled water and a cuddle. He was obviously not genuinely hungry as he had been in the past. Within a couple of weeks Edward would often stir between 5am and 6am but quickly settled back to sleep until 7am. I advised his parents to wait at least a month before bringing his solids back to 5pm. Once he was well established at going through to 7am and capable of taking more solids without this decreasing his last bottle too much, they could move his solids back to 5pm, followed by his bottle after the bath at 6.30pm.

Case History - Kate, aged five months

Problem: early-morning waking after solids were introduced

Cause: wrong types of food at the wrong time

Like Edward, Kate was sleeping through the night from her last feed at the age of eight weeks. Unlike Edward's parents, Kate's had followed the routines in *The Contented Little Baby Book* to the letter and had not dropped the 10pm milk until solids were established. She continued to sleep well from 7pm to 7am for a good three weeks after solids were introduced, then when she reached five months she suddenly started to wake up earlier and earlier. Like Edward, Kate would not settle back to sleep unless she was fed. Her mother could not understand why this was happening, as Kate was by this time established on three good solid meals a day and taking the right amount of milk at all her feeds.

With Edward's early-morning waking I could pinpoint immediately why things had gone wrong; this was not the case with Kate. I asked her mother, Caroline, to record the exact amounts and the types of food that Caroline was eating at each meal and forward it to me.

When I received the food diary, I saw that Kate was certainly taking good quantities of solids for her age and weight, plus the right amount of milk, but it was obvious that her diet was very low in carbohydrates. Lunch was a combination of three to four cubes of vegetables and tea was three cubes of either apple or pear purée, plus one teaspoon of baby rice mixed with a small amount of formula. Caroline was not convinced that low carbohydrate meals in the evening were the cause of Kate's early-morning waking, but when I asked her what she would choose to eat if she was really hungry at the end of the day, an apple or some rice pudding, she agreed to try altering Kate's meals. I advised Caroline to increase the baby rice gradually over a period of several days to three teaspoons mixed with milk, while reducing the pear purée to one cube. Once this was established, I suggested that Caroline try to combine at least one cube of a starch vegetable amongst Kate's lunchtime vegetables. I explained that a variety of fruit and vegetables is essential but they should be balanced with a carbohydrate such as baby rice or sweet potato, as these types of carbohydrate are what helps satisfy the baby's hunger. Within a few days Kate was back to sleeping soundly to 7am.

Over the last few years I have discovered a huge link between food and sleep. I believe that between five and nine months it is not just getting the quantities right that affects sleep, but also ensuring that the right foods are given at the right times.

I discuss how to structure weaning in more detail in my book *The Contented Little Baby Book of Weaning*.

Case Study – Jack, aged five months

Problem: feeding and crying all night

Cause: feeding on demand and wrong sleep associations

Jack's parents had read the book *Three in a Bed* and followed the advice of the author Deborah Jackson with their first child Jessica. Although Jessica did not have a strict routine she was a very happy and content little girl, and had moved out of her parents' bed and into her own room, happily, at around two years of age. When Jack was born his parents took the same approach as with his elder sister. He had slept in his parents' bed since birth and was breast fed on demand. However, contrary to claims by the author that co-sleeping and demand feeding always work, Jack was not a secure, happy and contented baby. By the time Jack had reached five months, both parents were at their wits' end trying to cope with a baby who was still waking and feeding several times a night and was fussy and fretful all day. By evening both parents were totally exhausted by trying to meet Jack's demands and they began to neglect the needs of his elder sister. Things eventually came to a head when the parents noticed a distinct change in their daughter's behaviour. Realising that sleep deprivation was beginning to affect every aspect of their family life, they contacted me for advice on how to get Jack to sleep by himself. They had already tried the gradual method of sleep-training with Jack, and things had actually got worse instead of better.

I suggested that they start by establishing a regular feeding and sleeping routine for Jack during the day, settling him in his cot awake for each sleep-time. Once Jack was settled in his cot, they were to use the controlled crying method to train him to sleep there.

The first evening, he cried the minute they put him in the cot. They used the checking method every five minutes and after 20 minutes he had fallen asleep.

His mother woke him at 11pm for a quick feed and, because she was worried about him crying and waking his sister, she resettled him with a dummy. She continued to put it in his mouth every time he cried until eventually he fell asleep at 5am. His mother woke him at 7am and, for the first time ever, he emptied both breasts. The next day I suggested that the parents try to settle Jack without the dummy since using it to get him to sleep would create a further problem. They were also to continue to extend the length of time between checks.

On the second day Jack was settled in his cot for all his naps without the dummy. He would cry for 5–15 minutes before going off to sleep. That evening he fell asleep after 20 minutes of crying and again had to be woken at 11pm for his feed. He settled quickly after that feed, slept until 4am and cried on and off until 5am, before going back to sleep till 6.30am.

By the end of the first week Jack's sleeping pattern was still quite erratic. However, he was settling well at 7pm with very little crying, only waking once or twice in the night. He usually managed to settle himself back to sleep within 10–20 minutes and his parents no longer needed to use the checking method. By the end of the second week he was waking only once in the night and settling himself back sleep within 5–10 minutes.

Jack was still being woken at 11pm to be fed and had begun cutting back on his morning feed, so I suggested not waking him for the 11pm feed. I was confident that he was feeding well with his solids, but advised his parents that if they continued to feed him at 11pm he might start to cut back even further on his morning milk feed and solids, then start to wake up genuinely hungry in the night.

For the next two nights he woke briefly at 1am but settled back within 10 minutes, sleeping through until 6.30am.

Sleep-training Jack took much longer than normal and
the parents had to go through 16 difficult and heart-
wrenching days and nights of controlled crying to train him
to sleep happily in his cot both during the day and at night.
However, he is now such a happy, content and relaxed baby
that they definitely believe it was the right thing to do.

Illness – the effect on sleep

The majority of my first-born babies managed to get through their
first year without suffering the usual colds and coughs that seemed
to plague my second- and third-born babies. By the time my first
babies experienced a cold, their sleep was so well established that
wakings in the night were very rare. With the second and third
babies this was not the case as they usually caught their first cold at
a much younger age from an elder brother or sister and disruptive
nights were inevitable. A baby under three months of age will usually
need help to get though the night when he has a cold or is ill. A
young baby with a cold can get very distressed, especially when he
is feeding, as he will not have learned to breathe through his mouth.

If your baby develops a cold or cough, regardless of how mild
it appears, he should be seen by a doctor. All too often I hear from
distressed parents of babies with serious chest infections, which
possibly could have been avoided if they had been seen by a doctor
earlier. Too many mothers delay taking their baby to the doctor,
worried that they be classed as neurotic, but it is important that you
discuss with your doctor any concerns you have about your baby's
health, no matter how small. If your baby is ill, it is essential that
your follow to the letter your doctor's advice, especially on feeding.

When a sick baby needs attention in the evening and during the
night, it should be given calmly and quietly. I believe that a sick baby
needs more rest than a healthy baby. Lots of visitors and activity
during the evening and in the night should be avoided. When I had to
care for a sick baby who was waking several times a night, I found it

less disruptive to the routine if I slept in the same room as the baby. It enabled me to attend to him quickly and I was less likely to disrupt the sleep of elder siblings by to-ing and fro-ing along the corridor.

Occasionally, I found that an older baby who had dropped night-time feeds would, once he had recovered, continue to wake up in the night looking for the same attention he received when he was unwell. For the first few nights I would check him and offer him some cool boiled water, but once I was convinced he was totally recovered, I would get tough and leave him to settle himself. In my experience, parents who are not prepared to do this usually end up with a baby who develops a long-term sleep problem.

Case Study – Freddy and Isabella, aged five months

Problem: excessive night-time waking and drinking
Cause: illness and wrong sleep associations

Freddy and Isabella were fed three-hourly when they were born. By the end of the second week their feeding and weight gain were so good that they could go on to the four-week routine described on page 74. Both babies continued to feed well and adapted easily to the gradual changes in the routine. By 12 weeks both babies were sleeping through to 7am from their last feed at 10pm. They did this consistently until they were four months old, when they both caught colds that quickly developed into chest infections.

Both babies began to wake several times a night because of difficulty in breathing. Their mother spent much of the night holding one baby or the other, as they only managed to sleep short spells before waking up in a dis-tressed state. Following advice from the doctor, they were offered fluids several times a night to avoid dehydration.

Unfortunately, once they were fully recovered, both babies continued to wake up two or three times a night and would not settle back to sleep without a cuddle and a drink. This pattern went on for nearly three weeks until sleep deprivation began to have a serious effect on the twins and their mother, who became physically and mentally exhausted from getting up several times a night and coping with two very tired, irritable babies during the day. The doctor advised her to try to break the twins' habit of waking at night by using the controlled crying method. She attempted this for two nights but found the five hours of continuous crying too hard to bear.

It was at this stage that she rang me in the hope that I knew of another method. I explained that the controlled crying method was the most effective way to treat this very common problem, but I suggested that it would probably work better if she implemented the core night method first, trying to eliminate the night-time wakings and drinks one at a time. The babies' waking times were fairly consistent: around 1am, 3am and 5am. I advised that she eliminate the waking at 1am first. This would be quite easy, as the babies were still having a small feed at 10pm. I advised her, on the first night, to wait until 11.45pm before feeding the babies. They both took nearly 150ml (5oz) at this time and settled back to sleep quickly. They slept through the usual waking time and woke at 2.15am. As planned, their mother checked them every 10–15 minutes but did not pick them up or speak to either of them. Both babies cried on and off for over an hour before waking again at 5am, This time the mother went straight to them and settled them back to sleep with a drink of well-diluted juice and a cuddle. They then slept until 7am.

The second night they both woke at around 2.45am. Their mother followed the same plan as the first night, only she extended the interval between checks to 20 minutes. They both cried on and off for just under one hour, settling back to sleep by 3.40am. They then woke at around

6.30am but were happy to lie in their cots until their mother went in at 7am to feed them.

On the third night we agreed that she should wait 30 minutes before going in to check them. Both babies slept through to 3.25am. Freddy cried for 10 minutes and then settled himself back to sleep, and Isabella cried for 35 minutes before settling herself back to sleep. Because Isabella's cry was calming down after 25 minutes, her mother decided not to go in to her after the 30 minutes. Both twins awoke around 6.50am.

The fourth night Freddy slept through to 7am and Isabella to 5am. She cried on and off for 40 minutes before settling herself back to sleep. As on the previous night, Isabella's crying was not very hard and her mother decided not to go in at all that night.

On the fifth night there was a lot of loud groaning between 5.30am and 6am but neither baby cried out and both had to be woken at 7am. They were fed at 11.45pm for a further two nights. As both babies continued to sleep through to 7am, I suggested that this feed should be brought forward by 10 minutes every couple of nights until they were back to feeding at 10pm.

I then advised the mother to reduce the amount they were fed at 10pm by 30ml (1oz) and if they continued to sleep through, to continue reducing it by a further 30ml (1oz) every three nights.

Within nine days the 10pm feed was reduced to 60ml (2oz). As both babies were sleeping through to 7am, I advised the mother to drop the feed altogether. The babies are nearly 20 months old now and both have continued to sleep well from 7pm to 7am every night.

4

The Older Baby –
Six to Twelve Months

What to expect

The majority of childcare experts are in agreement that by six months a baby is capable of getting through the night without milk feeds. At this stage a baby needs around 14 to 15 hours of sleep a day, divided between night-time sleep and day-time naps. Day-time sleep is usually made up of one short nap and one longer nap, although a baby who does not sleep longer than an hour at a time may need to have a short nap in the late afternoon to avoid getting over-tired at bedtime.

If your baby is still waking up in the night, it is advisable to look at what is happening during the day. How much your baby sleeps during the day and the amount of food he eats still play a big part in how well he will sleep at night.

What to aim for

The majority of babies are established on three solid meals a day during the sixth month. Once this happens, it is important that milk feeds are reduced to three a day. A baby having a full milk feed in the morning, followed by one around 2.30pm and one before bedtime will receive all the milk he needs to meet his nutritional needs. If you continue to feed your baby in the night, he will not increase his solids at the rate needed to satisfy his rapid growth. Between six and nine months many babies who had previously slept well start to wake up in the night because they are not taking the

right amount of solids for their age and weight. It is still very important to get the right balance between milk and solids. If your baby
has been sleeping through the night and is waking up earlier or in
the night it is advisable to take a close look at his feeding during
the day. For details of the right types of foods and quantities at this
stage check *The Contented Little Baby Book of Weaning*.

If your baby has never slept through the night and is still having
milk feeds in the night, you should gradually offer less and less or
dilute the feed down so that he feeds better during the day. Please
refer back to page 44 for advice on diluting feeds. Once the feeding
has been sorted out, you may still have to do some form of sleep-training, as night-time waking will have become a real habit by this stage.

Babies who are sleeping well to 7am will still need a short morning nap, but this should be pushed to nearer 9.30am, with the
lunchtime nap coming at around 12.30pm. I have observed that
parents who do not push this first nap on during the second part of
the first year, often end up with baby starting to wake earlier in the
morning. If your baby is sleeping well and has to be woken at 7am,
you can leave him to sleep later if this routine would fit in better. He
would not then need a morning nap, but may not manage to get
through to 12.30pm for his lunchtime nap. If this happens, try
bringing his lunch forward to 11.30am and put him down at
12.15pm for his lunchtime nap.

Between six and nine months the majority of babies start to roll
on to their front and move around the cot, often getting into a
tangle with the blankets. When this starts to happen it is better to
remove them altogether and put your baby into a sleeping bag, with
a tog rating suitable for the time of year.

If your baby is still waking in the night, it is possible that too
much day-time sleep is the cause of the problem. Check that he is
not sleeping more than three hours between 7am and 7pm and
remember that allowing your baby to sleep past 7am may be part of
the problem. A baby who is sleeping until 8am plus having a further
two naps in the day may be getting too much sleep. A typical day in
the life of a six- to twelve-month-old baby who is sleeping well at

night would look something like the routine below. If your baby is sleeping more during the day than the following routine suggests, try gradually cutting back on his day-time sleep. He may be irritable for a few days until he gets used to having less day-time sleep, but if too much day-time sleep is the cause of his night-time waking, cutting back should result in him sleeping better at night.

Between six and twelve months a typical day would look similar to the following:

7am	awake, milk feed followed by breakfast
9/9.30am	nap-time of no longer than 30–40minutes
11.30/12pm	lunch
12.30pm	nap-time – up to two hours
2.30/3pm	milk feed
4.30pm	short nap if he slept less than one hour at earlier nap
5pm	tea
6/6.30pm	bath and bedtime routine
7/7.30pm	asleep

The bedtime routine

If you have not already established a bedtime routine, follow the guidelines on page 23, but do so an hour prior to the time your baby or toddler is going to bed at present. After several nights of following the bathtime routine, you can gradually start to move it forward 10 or 20 minutes every few nights, until you reach the time you have decided that you want your baby or toddler to go to bed. Obviously if your baby or toddler is not sleeping well at night, you will probably have to implement some sort of sleep-training, but this should only be done once you are confident that you are getting his feeding right during the day. Attempting to sleep-train a baby or toddler who is not getting enough to eat at the right times during the day will more than likely end in failure.

Refer to the recommended routine for your baby's age and try to establish meal times at the given times and a bedtime routine suitable for his age before attempting sleep-training.

Common Problems

- Feeding
- Anxiety
- Moving around the cot (rolling over and standing up)
- Teething
- Early morning waking
- Comforter dependency

Feeding

If you are confident that you are getting your baby's day-time sleep right and that excessive napping is not the cause of night-time waking, the next area to look at is his feeding. Nearly 80 per cent of the sleeping problems that I have to deal with between the ages of six months and one year are caused by parents not getting the baby's feeding right. Feeding in the night at this stage will definitely affect the amount of solids a baby takes during the day, and getting the right amount of solids balanced with the correct amount of milk is vital. Increasing solids too rapidly during the day also can cause problems as it can result in too small a milk feed at bedtime. Excessive amounts of fruit and vegetables late afternoon causing the baby to poo in the middle of the night is a another problem – usually linked to the baby not getting enough protein. Feeding your baby too much commercially prepared food also results in a low intake of protein, a further cause of night-time waking.

Case Study – David, aged seven months

Problem: excessive night-time feeding

Cause: fed too much convenience food

David, who was bottle-fed from birth, would wake up screaming every hour and a half in the night, and was fretful and miserable for most of the day. When he was three months old, his exhausted parents decided to try the contented little baby routines. They later admitted to being both suspicious and sceptical about my advice and techniques, because they contradicted nearly all of the advice in the other books that they had consulted. However, as the other advice hadn't worked, desperation led them to follow my routines to the letter. Within three days David was sleeping through the night and had become a happy and contented baby during the day. This pattern continued for two months.

Then, when David outgrew his Moses basket at five months of age, his parents decided that they would move his 20-month-old sister Andrea into a bed and give her cot to David. He continued to sleep well when moved to the big cot, but the move from a cot to a bed for Andrea turned out to be a disaster and resulted in weeks of hysterical crying and sleepless nights.

While the situation with Andrea was becoming steadily worse, exhaustion led her mother to neglect David's diet and routine. He was given jars of baby food rather than the fresh food that had been an essential part of his dietary requirements. She also started to cut out his bath and massage in the evening. Soon David started to wake up every night at around 10pm and would not settle back without a feed, even though he had dropped this feed a good six weeks previously. Worse still, he started to wake up when his sister was crying in the night. His mother ended up giving him a formula feed in the night so that he would settle back quickly and allow her to return to a hysterical Andrea.

This excessive night-time feeding resulted in David eating even fewer solids than usual. He would take only a small amount of cereal after his morning bottle – about two tablespoonfuls at lunchtime, and two teaspoonfuls of baby rice mixed with milk at teatime. This was too little and did not include any form of protein, which is essential for a baby aged seven months and weighing 17lbs.

Although she was exhausted trying to deal with two sleepless children, David's mother followed my advice and made two batches of chicken and vegetable casserole and two batches of lentil and vegetable casserole. Within two days of introducing this food at lunchtime, David began to drink less in the night. She gradually increased his lunchtime solids to six tablespoonfuls of chicken or lentil casserole, and his teatime baby rice from two teaspoonfuls to six teaspoonfuls mixed with a couple of tablespoonfuls of either fruit or vegetable purée. These amounts were much more realistic for a baby of David's age and weight. Although he continued to wake for a further four nights at 10pm, his mother was able to settle him back to sleep with a small drink of cool boiled water. Within a further three nights David was back to sleeping from 7pm to 7am.

I believe that the main cause of David's sudden nighttime waking was genuine hunger caused by not receiving the correct amounts of the right sort of food for his age and weight. In my experience the occasional use of convenience food is fine, but babies who are being fed constantly from jars and packets are much more likely to develop sleep problems related to feeding.

Anxiety

By the age of six months babies begin to realise they are separate from their mothers and may show signs of separation anxiety or stranger anxiety. The happy contented baby who was so easy-going and relaxed and who would go to anyone suddenly becomes clingy, anxious and demanding.

He screams if his mother leaves the room for even a few minutes and often gets hysterical if approached by a stranger. Some babies will even get upset when relations they know well attempt to talk to them or pick them up. This behaviour is a totally normal part of the baby's development. All babies go through this stage to some degree between the age of six and twelve months, and it is usually around nine months that it becomes most obvious. In my experience, babies who are used to being with someone else on a regular basis usually suffer less from separation anxiety.

If your baby suddenly becomes more clingy around this age, it is important to understand that he is not being naughty or demanding. Forcing him to go to strangers or leaving him alone in a room to play by himself will not solve the problem and may lead to him becoming more fretful and insecure. Because this stage often coincides with the time a mother returns to work, a baby who has always slept well at night can start to wake up in the night fretful and anxious. Responding quickly and positively to his anxiety rather than ignoring it will, in the long run, help him to become more confident and independent. However, it is important that you do not give your baby so much attention that he begins to feel that he is being rewarded for his night-time waking.

Although this stage can be very exhausting for a mother, it rarely lasts long. The following guidelines can help make this difficult period less stressful and hopefully keep any sudden night-time waking to a minimum.

- If you are planning to return to work when your baby is between six and twelve months, it is important that he gets accustomed to being left with someone else for short spells before he reaches six months of age. He should be gradually left for longer and longer periods until he is happy to be left for the length of time you will be separated once you go back to work. Ideally, he should have had a settling in period with the childminder or nursery of a month – and a minimum of two weeks – before you go back to work.

- It is also important to get him used to large groups and new experiences long before you start back at work. Try to arrange regular play dates with a small group of the same mothers and babies. Once he appears to be happy and responding to the regular faces, increase the number of people and vary the venues.

• Provided you are confident that your baby is happy with his carer, do not prolong the goodbye. A hug and a reminder that you will be back soon is enough. Using the same approach and words each time you say goodbye will, in the long-term, be more reassuring than going back to try to calm him.

• During this period instruct your baby's carer that he must not be subjected to too many different new things at once or to handling by strangers. The calmer and more predictable his routine, the more quickly he will get over his feelings of anxiety.

• Between nine and twelve months many babies develop a need for a comforter at sleep-times, usually a special blanket, cloth or toy. If you do decide to give your baby a comforter in his bed, it is important that you allow him to have it only at nap-times and that he is not allowed to drag it around during the day. It is also a good idea to purchase a duplicate to allow for frequent washing or in case it becomes damaged or lost.

Case Study – Holly, aged nine months

Problem: sudden night-time waking

Cause: separation anxiety when sent to childminder

Holly was a first baby and her parents had implemented a routine from the first week. She was sleeping from 7.30pm to 7am with a feed at 10pm from nine weeks of age, and at five months she dropped the late feed and was sleeping right through. Apart from the couple of times she had had a cold, she had never woken in the night. Because her mother Julie knew that she would be going back to work when Holly was eight months old, she made a conscious decision not to get involved with the many mother and baby activities in the area. She felt that the little time that she was going to have with Holly was very precious and that she wanted to spend as much time as possible with Holly on a one-to-one basis. Therefore meetings with other mothers and babies were kept to a minimum and the only time that Holly was left with anyone for short spells was during her nap-times. Julie would always settle Holly for her nap and make sure that she was back in time to get Holly up.

When Holly reached five and a half months, her mother realised that she would have to start to look for some sort of childcare for when she returned to work. This proved more difficult than she had envisaged and it was over two months before she managed to find a suitable childminder – which meant that Holly and the childminder had only two weeks to get to know each other. For the first week Julie would drop Holly off in the morning and spend a short time with her and the childminder. By the end of the second week Holly was being left alone with the childminder between 8am and 2pm. She would get very upset when Julie dropped her off in the morning and look very tired and red-eyed when her mother picked her up in the afternoon. The childminder assured Julie that this was very normal and that things would get better within a couple of weeks. Julie returned to work on the third week and Holly was left from 8am to 5pm with the childminder. By the fourth week, things were deteriorating. Holly had always enjoyed her solids at teatime and her bathtime routine, but now she began to get very fussy and fretful. She started to eat less and less at teatime and cried throughout her bath. The last breast feed of the day had always been a very quiet relaxing one, but this too became very difficult. Holly would scream and thrash around and keep pulling off the breast. This behaviour would last for over an hour, when Holly would eventually fall asleep exhausted, but not having taken a full feed. She then began to wake up earlier and earlier in the morning looking for a feed. Because Holly hadn't fed well in the evening, Julie felt she was genuinely hungry and would feed her. By the time Holly reached nine months, things had got worse. She would wake up to two or three times a night and often would not settle back without a feed. She became more and more clingy at weekends and in the evenings, and it got that her mother could not leave the room for a minute without Holly getting hysterical. Things had not improved with the childminder and Holly would cry hysterically when dropped off there in the morning, and be red-eyed and fretful when picked up in the evening.

When Julie rang me for help, I asked her to forward me a feeding and sleeping diary for the day with the childminder. Julie confessed that because Holly had always been in such a good routine and was so predictable with her eating, she had not asked the childminder to keep one. It did not surprise me that she did not think that it was necessary; however, it did ring alarm bells that as a professional carer the childminder had not automatically kept one. Julie assured me that the childminder was registered and came with the highest recommendations. She had worked as a nursery nurse and now had a little boy of her own aged two years, and looked after another little boy of 18 months four days a week. She also looked after a five-year-old between 3.30pm and 5pm every day. I asked Julie if she had actually spent time with the childminder and Holly when all the other children were around. She confessed that she hadn't. Although I couldn't be sure, I suspected that there were a number of different reasons

for Holly's behaviour, the main one being that the childminder was probably not that experienced in caring for
such a young baby. Although she had worked as a nursery
nurse, it was very possible that she specialised in toddlers
and older children, and apart from her own child had no
experience of dealing with the separation anxiety of a baby
Holly's age.

I felt that to get to the root of the problem it was essential for Julie to spend a whole day with the childminder to
see what was happening with Holly's feeding and sleeping. Julie felt very uneasy about doing this, as she was
afraid it could imply to the childminder that she was not
doing her job properly.

I reassured Julie that if the childminder was a true professional she would be keen to resolve the problem and
not be offended at the suggestion. It was agreed that the
following day Julie would tell the childminder that she
would like to spend some time observing Holly. She would
reassure her that under no circumstances would she inter-
vene in the care of Holly but would explain the importance
of resolving the problem of Holly's fretfulness and night
wakings. By the time a very tearful Julie rang me that
evening to go through the day's events, she had already
written her resignation and sacked the childminder.

True to her word, she had not intervened at all throughout the day, but as she relayed to me what had happened,
it became very obvious why Holly was so fretful and
unhappy.

The day had started with a trip to a local playgroup –
obviously with two toddlers to care for the childminder
could not be expected to sit at home all day. However,
according to Julie, the minute they arrived at the church
hall where the group took place, Holly became fretful. The
hall was packed with mothers, babies and very noisy toddlers – something that Holly was quite unused to. The

childminder struggled to control two very boisterous little boys and calm Holly down. Lots of well-meaning mothers came up and gave advice on how best to deal with a very hysterical Holly. She was passed from one to the other, and was burped, rocked, sung to and offered juice to try to calm her down. Eventually she fell asleep exhausted in her buggy after drinking a huge amount of juice from a bottle. She dozed on and off for the remainder of the play date, which lasted about one and a half hours.

When they got back to the childminder's house she woke up crying. She was then offered more juice to calm her down, so that the childminder could prepare the two boys' food. Once they were eating their meal, the child-minder started to try to feed Holly. She fussed and fretted throughout the meal and the childminder put this behaviour down to teething. But Julie realised that Holly had been given far too much juice that morning to eat a good lunch.

At around 1pm Holly was rocked to sleep in her buggy. The childminder explained that they were due to visit a friend that afternoon so there was no point in settling Holly in her cot. Holly slept around 45 minutes and awoke crying just minutes before they arrived at the childminder's friend's house. She was then given a 270ml (9oz) bottle of formula by the friend, which was a good 90ml (3oz) more than she was used to drinking when her mother had cared for her. Three other mothers and their children arrived soon after and another very noisy play date took place, Holly again being passed around from person to person to try to keep her calm. At 4pm she started to get extremely fret-ful and was offered another large drink of juice and a couple of chocolate biscuits.

By 4.30pm Julie could no longer bear watching her once calm and happy little baby getting so upset made an excuse and left. What had become very obvious was the reason for Holly's sudden refusal to eat at teatime. She had been given enormous amounts of juice and much more milk than she needed, resulting in her poor appetite in the evening.

Such a dramatic change to her daily routine and having to cope with such a huge increase in mental and physical stimulation from so many different people was more than Holly could cope with at a stage when she was already fretful about being parted from her mother.

Fortunately, Julie's employers were very understanding about the problem and allowed her to take a couple of months' leave to try to sort out more suitable childcare arrangements.

I explained to Julie that all babies suffer from separation anxiety to some degree at this stage and future care of Holly must be planned very carefully if the same problem were not to occur again.

Julie spent a month at home getting Holly back into a good routine and looking for another childminder. I advised her to choose someone who had only one or two older children in her care and to get Holly used to her very gradually. She should also spend different parts of the day with her over several days, so that childminder understood Holly's routine. Fortunately, the next childminder was slightly older with a much calmer lifestyle and Holly relaxed fairly quickly with her.

Over a period of six weeks Holly was left for longer and longer periods each day, and by the time she reached her first birthday she would happily wave goodbye to her mother in the morning and greet her with a smile in the evening.

Much of all this anguish could have been avoided if Julie had got Holly used to being left with someone else at a much younger age. Getting her used to larger playgroups earlier on would also have helped prepare her for the more hectic and lively environment that is to be expected at any nursery or childminder's.

Rolling over

Between the ages of six and nine months the majority of babies start to roll from their back to their front and, until they learn to roll back on to their back, they can get quite upset. You may find that for a few weeks you have to help them resettle back to sleep by rolling them back. To avoid this becoming a long-term habit, help your baby practise rolling backwards and forwards during his play-time. Once your baby has become confident about rolling back and forth from his tummy to his back, it is advisable not to rush to him the minute he cries out. Allow him a short spell to settle himself, otherwise he will become dependent on you to help him get back to sleep. Also, once he has become very mobile in the cot it is a good idea to get him used to going down for some of his day-time naps on his tummy. Once he is happy to sleep in any position, I would advise putting him in a sleeping bag if you have not already done so, and removing the top sheet and any blankets. This will avoid the problem of him kicking the blankets off and getting cold in the night or getting into a tangle with the bedding.

Standing up

Between nine and twelve months some babies will start pulling themselves up in the cot, but will not be able to get themselves back down to the sleeping position. Again, they will need some help getting back down until they have learned to do it themselves. As with rolling over, a long-term dependency can set in if you do not teach your baby how to get himself back down. It is a good idea when settling him at sleep-time to put him in the cot standing and, holding his hands, teach him how to hold on to the bars and lower himself down to whatever sleeping position he prefers.

Teething

In my experience, babies who enjoy a routine from a very early age and have established healthy sleeping habits are rarely bothered by teething. I have found that babies who have suffered from colic or have developed poor sleeping habits are more likely to wake in the night when they are teething. However, some babies who normally sleep well do wake up for a short spell when the molars are coming through.

If you feel that your baby's night-time wakings are caused by severe teething pain, I suggest you seek advice from your doctor regarding the use of paracetamol. While genuine teething pain may cause a few disruptive nights, it should never last for several weeks.

If your baby is teething and waking in the night but quickly settles back to sleep when given a cuddle or a dummy, teething is probably not the cause of the waking. A baby who is genuinely bothered by teething pain will be difficult to settle back to sleep. He will also show signs of discomfort during the day, not just at night. It is advisable to look for other reasons for his night-time waking.

Once a feeding problem has been eliminated, I find that another common cause of night waking is the baby kicking off his covers. Many parents who have contacted me for advice on teething and night-time waking, report an immediate improvement when they put their baby in a sleeping bag at night.

Early-morning waking

All babies will come into a light sleep between 5 and 6am. During the first few months the cause is often hunger and the majority will settle back to sleep until nearer 7am when given a quick quiet feed.

Between six and twelve months nearly all babies are well established on three solid meals a day and three milk feeds. Provided a baby is receiving the right balance of protein, carbohydrates, vegetables and fruit, plus three full milk feeds a day, he should not be waking up because he is hungry. In my experience, once hunger is ruled out one of the main reasons for early morning waking is that the day-time sleep is not properly structured. I receive many calls from parents who say that their baby has been sleeping until 7am for many months but now, between six and twelve months, is waking up earlier and earlier. In many of these cases the problem has evolved because the parents did not move the day-time naps forward. A baby who is sleeping well until 7am at six months should, by the time he reaches nine months, manage to stay awake until nearer 9.30am. This would mean that the middle of the day sleep would be pushed on to 12.30/1.00pm. The early waking, however, has the knock-on effect of the baby needing to go down early for his first nap of the day and a vicious circle soon emerges. Babies whose naps have been gradually moved later tend to go into their cot tired but usually chattering or singing for a short spell before going off to sleep. I am sure it is because they are going down less tired and drift into a light sleep later that they sleep longer in the morning.

If your baby is starting to wake up earlier, and earlier try gradually moving his first nap of the day forward by five minutes every three or four days so that he will eventually be happy to go down later for his middle of the day nap.

The other main reason for early-morning waking is that parents have established a longer morning nap. During the first six months this longer nap does not usually affect the mornings, as the majority of babies will still be having quite a long nap in the afternoon. However, during the second part of the first year all babies will begin to cut back on their day-time sleep. If they cut back on their afternoon nap this will cause over-tiredness at bedtime again and the same vicious circle as already described. If your baby is waking early and sleeping one to two hours in the morning and only one hour in the afternoon, gradually cut back on his morning nap by 10 minutes every three to four days, until he is sleeping no more than 30–40 minutes. This should have the knock-on effect of him sleeping longer in the afternoon. If for some reason he will only sleep an hour or less at the second nap, try offering him a small drink of milk, water or well diluted juice before he goes down, in case thirst is preventing him from sleeping longer at this time.

Comforter dependency

Between six and nine months nearly all babies begin to develop an attachment to a comforter. The choice of comforter varies from baby to baby. Some become dependent on a blanket or muslin; others may choose a soft toy or use their thumb or a dummy. Psychologists believe the use of a comforter occurs around the age that babies realise they are an individual person, separate from their mother. These transitional comfort objects give a baby or toddler a sense of security when they feel alone or vulnerable. Baby and childcare expert Penelope Leach says that something cuddly is thought to be a 'stand-in' for the mother as a comfort object, which the baby or child can use when the mother is not available to him.

The majority of experts agree that use of a comforter is a normal part of a baby's development, but most stress the importance of a child not becoming over-dependent on it. This can easily be avoided if comforters are restricted to rest times and sleep-times. Allowing a baby to drag a muslin, blanket or toy around everywhere can lead to disaster if the item in question gets lost.

By three years of age most children become less reliant on their comforter and have usually abandoned it altogether by the time they reach five years.

The following guidelines can help avoid overdependency, which can lead to problems later on.

- When you notice your baby or toddler becoming attached to a certain object, limit its use to bedtime or special rest time in the house. Do not allow him to drag it from room to room or on trips out – though obviously you will need to take it on holidays and overnight visits. Otherwise be insistent that the blanket, muslin or toy stays in the cot.

- If possible, try to purchase a duplicate, as this will allow frequent washing and provide you with a replacement if the comforter becomes damaged or lost.

• If you find that your young baby or toddler is getting more and more dependent on a comforter and is withdrawn and not interacting in the way that he used to, there could be some underlying emotional reason.

Case Study – Felix, aged seven months

Problem: waking in the night and refusing to settle without feeding

Cause: imbalance of solids causing him to poo in the night

Felix weighed nearly 10lb at birth and for the first month demanded to be breast-fed two-hourly during the day and three-hourly in the night. By the time he reached six weeks he weighed nearly 12lb and was beginning to demand feed every two hours during the night as well as during the day. With a toddler of 18 months to also care for, his mother Alexis was becoming exhausted and decided to introduce a bottle of formula at 10pm to see if it would help Felix in the night. Although things did improve, Felix continued to wake up twice in the night demanding to be fed, and by the time he reached 14 weeks he weighed over 16lb. Reluctant to wean him before four months, Alexis decided to switch from breast feeding to formula feeding. By 16 weeks Felix was being totally formula-fed and was happily going four hours during the day and sleeping to nearer 5am in the morning from his 10pm feed. At four months Alexis tried to introduce a small amount of baby rice, but after the first mouthful Felix would scream and clamp his lips shut, refusing to take any more.

Felix now weighed around 18lb and Alexis realised that being such a big baby he would be unlikely to drop his middle of the night feed until he was taking some solids.

A friend suggested that she add a small amount of fruit

to the baby rice to make it more palatable. This seemed to have the desired effect and within a few days Felix was happily taking his solids. As he increased the amount of solids he was taking, he gradually started to sleep longer and longer in the night, and by the time he had reached 20 weeks he was on solids three times a day and sleeping through until 6.30am from his last feed at 10pm. As his solids increased during the day, he started to cut back on his 10pm feed and at 22 weeks he was sleeping from 7pm to 6.30am. He continued with this sleep pattern for nearly four weeks when suddenly, at six and a half months, he started to wake up in the night having done a poo. Alexis would quickly change his nappy and try to settle him with some cool boiled water. Because he was taking four full formula feeds a day plus eight to ten tablespoonfuls of solids three times a day, Alexis was convinced he wasn't waking because of hunger in the night and, at nearly seven months, she felt that he should be capable of sleeping through without a feed.

However, Felix became more and more difficult to re-settle after his nappy change and would cry on and off most of the night. One night, in desperation, Alexis resorted to feeding Felix again. He drank nearly 240ml (8oz) in 10 minutes and settled back to sleep until 7am. Over the next few nights Alexis fed Felix but followed the advice in Richard Ferber's book, *Solve Your Child's Sleep Problems*, for babies over six months. She gradually reduced the amount of formula powder she was putting in the bottle and by the fourth night she was offering Felix half-strength feed after his first waking in the night. However, this plan resulted in Felix waking a second time around 5am with another dirty nappy.

It was at this stage that Alexis rang me, having tried controlled crying and diluted feeds, she was desperate.

It was obvious that the main cause of Felix's waking

was a dirty nappy, and until we found the reason for him pooing in the night I advised Alexis to give Felix a full-strength feed, as I believed that the second waking in the night with a dirty nappy was definitely being caused by the diluted feed.

Over the next few days Felix went back to waking only once in the night, and once his nappy was changed he would settle straight back to sleep when given a 240ml (8oz) full-strength feed.

Unlike most babies of this age who take a large milk feed in the night, Felix did not cut back on his day-time eating. He would still take four full formula feeds a day and continued to eat an enormous amount of solids. I asked Alexis to keep a very detailed diary of the exact quantities of the different foods that Felix was eating and how many dirty nappies he had during the day.

After several more days it became very clear to me that although Felix was eating an enormous amount of food, his appetite was not being satisfied. Hence the middle of the night feed did not take the edge off his day-time eating. On studying his eating plan more closely, it became evident that he was not eating nearly enough carbohydrates or protein for his age and size, and was eating far too much fruit and vegetables. I sent Alexis several recipes for Felix's protein meals which I advised her to follow as they contained the right amount of chicken for his age and weight. I also advised her that, apart from bananas, she should give Felix fruit only at breakfast time. We also increased his carbohydrates at breakfast and at teatime, and if he was still hungry after lunch I suggested that Alexis give him a small rice cake instead of his usual fruit.

Within two days Felix was down to doing a poo in the morning after breakfast and usually one more late afternoon. Although he still woke in the night he did not have a dirty nappy and could be settled with much less milk. I felt confident that, now that his day-time solids were sorted out, we could start diluting the middle of the night milk feed again. Alexis put only four scoops into his 150ml (5oz) bottle of water for the next two nights and he continued to sleep through to 7am. For the next two nights we reduced it to three scoops, and then to two scoops in 150ml (5oz) on the fifth night.

Felix got quite upset that night: he obviously tasted the difference in the diluted milk and he took a while to settle back to sleep, after only taking 60ml (2oz) of the diluted feed. Because he had to be woken at 7am, I advised Alexis to not rush to him when he woke that night, to see if he would settle himself. When he woke up he cried hard for about 10 minutes, then went quiet for five minutes before crying hard again for a further 10 minutes. Alexis was just about to go in to check him when he went quiet, this time for nearly 15 minutes. He had one more hard cry for 10 minutes, before settling himself back to sleep until 7am. The following night a similar pattern was repeated but lasted only 20 minutes. The third night Alexis heard a slight stirring a couple of times in the night, but no crying. Felix had to be woken at 7am that morning. He continued to sleep well from 7pm to between 6.30am or 7am in the morning.

Case Study – Thomas, aged six months

Problem: waking several times a night

Cause: excessive milk feeding

Thomas weighed nearly 10lb at birth and was breast fed on demand for the first three months. At four months he weighed nearly 17lb and was weaned on to formula. He was drinking approximately 210ml (7oz) every 3–3½ hours, well in excess of 1440ml (48oz) each day. At least two of these feeds were in the middle of the night. His mother, exhausted from getting up twice in the night to feed Thomas and concerned about his excessive milk intake, approached her health visitor for advice. The health visitor advised her to introduce solids at four months and reassured her that Thomas's milk feed would reduce once solids were established. She started Thomas on a small amount of baby rice at the 2pm feed. He took only a couple of mouthfuls and started to scream. He responded the same way the following day and, in desperation to get him to take the rice, she mixed it with half a jar of fruit purée.

Although he still protested, he did take a few teaspoonfuls. Over the weeks that followed, Thomas was offered a variety of fruit and vegetables. His response was always the same. He would take a few teaspoonfuls, then start to cry.

By five months Thomas was still waking and feeding in the night but now he was more difficult to settle back to sleep, often crying on and off until the next feed. Because the crying was accompanied by much hand chewing, his mother assumed that he was teething. At six months the crying and constant hand chewing were such a problem that she rang me for advice.

I suggested that during the following two days she write down complete details of Thomas's feeding, sleeping and crying. When I received these details it was immediately clear to me that the cause of the excessive crying and chewing was hunger, not teething.

Thomas now weighed over 19lb and was eating only two or three teaspoonfuls of fruit at breakfast, a couple of cubes of vegetables at lunchtime and four teaspoonfuls of baby rice in the evening. Because he was still feeding in the night, his daily intake of milk was so excessive that he was not increasing his solids during the day. Although the amount of food required varies from baby to baby, the quantity of solids Thomas was consuming was very low for his size.

To increase the amount of solids he was eating, his mother would have to reduce his milk intake very quickly. I suggested that for the next two days she eliminate the 2pm milk feed and replace it with well-diluted juice. This would cause Thomas to be hungrier at 5pm and eat more solids. The increase in solids would help reduce his middle of the night feeds. We also agreed that Thomas should be fed only once in the night. At all other wakings he should be offered water or well-diluted juice if he would not settle quickly.

The first evening he took an extra teaspoonful of baby rice and slept past his usual 11pm waking, sleeping until 1.30am. His mother offered him some cool boiled water, which he absolutely refused. She then offered some very well diluted juice, which he drank before settling back to sleep until 5am. As he had already dropped two feeds that night, she offered him a full 240ml (8oz) milk feed. He then settled back until 7am.

The second day he increased his lunchtime solids to three cubes of vegetables, and in the evening took 5½ teaspoons of baby rice mixed with milk. That night he slept through until 3am and settled back to sleep until 7am after being offered a drink of well diluted juice. Because he had cut out three night feeds in two days, I advised his mother to re-introduce a very small milk feed at 2pm to ensure his daily milk intake reached the minimum 600ml (20oz) recommended by health authorities.

Over the next four nights Thomas woke once somewhere between 3am and 5am, drank his well-diluted juice and settled back to sleep until 7am.

By the seventh day Thomas was eating a small amount of breakfast cereal after his morning formula feed and having four cubes of vegetable and chicken casserole at lunchtime with his formula feed. He then had a small formula feed at 2pm, and in the evening he was having six teaspoons of baby rice and two cubes of fruit purée after his formula feed.

That night he slept through from 7pm to 7am. I advised his mother that it was very important to keep decreasing his lunchtime milk feed and to increase his solids in order to meet his growing appetite and nutritional requirements. When he was down to only 90ml (3oz) of formula and his solids had increased to six to seven cubes of chicken and vegetable casserole, the lunchtime milk feed should then be dropped, and replaced with a drink of water or well diluted juice from a beaker. The 2pm milk could be increased, but this should be done gradually to ensure that he didn't overfeed and then not want his tea. His tea should be gradually increased to eight teaspoonfuls of baby rice, mixed with some formula and a small amount of fruit or vegetable purée.

By the time Thomas had reached seven months he was enjoying three well balanced meals a day, from a wide variety of foods, plus drinking the correct amount of milk for his age. He continued to sleep well at night and all the crying and hand chewing had disappeared.

Case Study – Ruby, aged ten months

Problem: early-morning waking

Cause: naps at wrong time of day

Although Ruby's parents did not follow the contented little baby routines, she slept through the night from four months, and had regular day-time naps. She went to bed around 7.30pm and would sleep soundly until 7/7.30am in the morning. Her mother worked from home and from very early on had encouraged Ruby to sleep longer in the morning. This enabled her to get all of her work done in the morning, keeping the afternoon free to take Ruby to different activities. Ruby would go down for a nap around 9.30am for a couple of hours, awake and have lunch, then have a second nap of approximately 40 minutes in her buggy or the car, while her mother and she were out and about. This routine worked very well until Ruby started to cut back on her late-afternoon nap at nine months. As the late afternoon nap got shorter and shorter, Ruby began to get tired much earlier in the evening.

By 6pm she was very irritable and it was a struggle for her mother to keep her awake until 7.30pm.

After a couple of weeks of getting only 20 minutes sleep after 11.30am, Ruby was so tired by 6pm that she was having to go to bed by 6.45pm, when she would fall into a deep sleep very quickly.

This resulted in her starting to wake up earlier and earlier in the morning, and by the end of the third week Ruby was waking up at 5.30/6am and refusing to go back to sleep. Because she was waking so early she started to get very tired long before 9.30am and would fall asleep between 8.30am and 9am, sleeping her usual two hours, but waking up earlier, around 11am. Her mother would try very hard to get Ruby to have a further nap of 30–40 minutes in the afternoon, often driving Ruby around for one to two hours at a time to try to induce sleep. This rarely worked and Ruby would usually sleep no more than 15–20 minutes. By the time she reached 10 months she was waking at 5am, refusing to go back to sleep and needing to nap at 8.30am. She rarely enjoyed her activities in the afternoon as she was so tired and her mother was exhausted with having to start the day so early and spend much of it with a very fretful and irritable baby.

When she rang for help, I explained that the problem was very common amongst babies who are allowed to establish a longer nap in the morning. Between nine and twelve months babies to tend to cut down their day-time sleep, and if that happens to be the sleep after 12 noon, the result is a very tired baby who needs to go to bed much earlier and usually falls into a very deep sleep too early. This has the knock-on effect of the baby waking up earlier and a vicious circle evolving as had happened with Ruby. I advised her mother that the only way we could resolve the problem was by gradually reducing the length of the morning nap and hoping that Ruby would begin to sleep earlier and longer at the next nap.

We cut down her morning sleep by 10 minutes every day for the first week, until she was sleeping just under one hour. By the end of the week Ruby was starting to need a nap much earlier in the afternoon, usually around 2pm, and would sleep for up to an hour. She then managed to stretch to 7pm at bedtime, although she was still going into a deep sleep very quickly.

By the second week we had managed to push her morning nap to around 9am and cut back very hard, allowing her only 30 minutes. She was then ready to sleep at around 12 noon and I advised her mother to make sure that for the next few weeks this middle of the day nap was in her cot, not in the buggy, to ensure that she got a proper rest. The first few days she slept just over an hour and would not take a short nap later in the day, so was still very tired by 7pm. However, by the third week she was sleeping nearer two hours and was not going into her cot so tired in the evening, often chattering for 10–15 minutes before going to sleep. Her mother would hear her stir and often chat for 20 minutes or so around 5.30am/6am, but she did not go to her, and more often than not she would go back to sleep until 7am. By the end of the month Ruby was sleeping 7.15pm to 7/7.30am at night and having 20–30 minutes in the morning and a good two hours every lunchtime.

Her mother had to alter her working hours to fit in with Ruby's lunchtime nap, but she felt that the sacrifice was well worth it.

Case Study – Megan, aged 12 months

Problem: waking several times a night

Cause: standing up

Megan had always slept well but at the age of 10 months suddenly started to wake up two or three times a night. Her parents would find her standing up at the end of the cot crying. They realised that although she was able to pull herself up to a standing position using the spars of the cot, she had not learned how to get herself down again. They would lay her down and quickly leave the room, and within minutes she would settle herself back to sleep. The same pattern would happen at least one more time in the night and, more often than not, twice more.

At around 11 months Megan, who had been cruising around the furniture since nine months, started walking. Although she was small, she was very steady on her feet and she quickly learned how climb up and down from the sofa. When her parents realised that she was capable of doing this, they decided to get tough about going in to help her lie back down in the middle of the night.

On the first night they decided that they would check her every 10 minutes from when she first woke up but they would not help her to lie back down. Megan cried on and off for over half an hour and her parents checked her three times, but each time left the room with her still standing at the bottom of the cot. Then, after about 45 minutes, Megan's cry suddenly went from whingy to hysterical. Her parents, realising that something was seriously wrong, rushed in to find her lying flat on her back, with the side of her face jammed up against the cot spars and one of her arms twisted around the spar. She must have somehow lost her balance and fallen backwards against the spars, trapping her arm as she fell and causing her face to bang against the side of the cot.

She was obviously very distressed and it took over an hour of cuddling and a drink of juice to calm her down. The following day a huge bruise appeared on the side of her face, making her already guilty parents feel even worse. That night when she woke they resumed their previous pattern of going straight to Megan and helping her to lie down. Only now she would not always settle straight back to sleep and more often than not had to be given a cuddle along with a drink of juice before she would lie down happily. Because Megan had always slept well, the disruptive nights and loss of sleep were beginning to affect her temperament during the day. She was very irritable and would cry for the least little thing, often throwing a complete tantrum if she did not get her own way. This pattern went on for a further month before her parents contacted me. They realised that they had to do something to solve the problem but were not keen to leave Megan to cry because of their bad experience when they had tried leaving her previously.

I explained that many parents went through a period when they had to go in and help their baby lie back down but I had rarely heard of this happening two or three times a night; it was more likely to happen near morning when the baby came into a light sleep. When I asked about Megan's day-time naps, her parents told me that she had always slept well, and was still having 45 minutes in the morning and up to two and a half hours at lunchtime. I was sure that the reason Megan was waking and standing up so often in the night was partly due to her parents not cutting back her day-time sleep.

Between nine and twelve months the majority of babies cut down on the amount of sleep they need, and parents should always look at the amount of day-time sleep their baby is having if there is a change in the night-time pattern.

I advised Megan's parents to continue to help her to settle in the night when they found her standing up, but at nap-times and in the evening they should put her in the cot and by holding her hands on the spars help her to get down to her sleeping position. It was important that they helped her but, as she became more capable, assisted her less and less.

I also suggested that they cut her morning nap back to 30 minutes for the next three days, and then cut her lunch-time nap back to a strict two hours. Within days of cutting down her day-time sleep, Megan was only waking up and pulling herself up twice in the night. By the end of the first week Megan was also lowering herself down to her sleeping position without any help from her parents. I then advised her parents that they should now adopt the same procedure in the night as they had at nap-times and in the evening. For several nights they should assist Megan to get down, then gradually help less and less. At the end of the second week they would go in and stand by the cot and tell Megan to lie down but not help her. It took a further week before Megan stopped calling out for her parents in the night.

Whether she was standing up and getting herself back down or just not getting up at all we weren't sure, but everyone was getting a good night's sleep and Megan went back to being a very happy little girl during the day.

When this problem first arises, parents should immediately start to teach their baby to lower himself when put in the cot, so that a long-term dependency does not develop. It is also important to look at how much sleep a baby is having during the day, as too much will result in him having much more energy in the night when he comes into his light sleep.

5
The Toddler – Twelve to Twenty-four Months

What to expect

During the first part of the second year the amount of sleep that a toddler needs begins to reduce. Up until one year most babies are still sleeping an average of 14–15 hours a day, divided between night-time sleep and two day-time naps. Between 12 and 18 months this is normally reduced to 13–14 hours a day, which is usually divided between night-time sleep and one day-time nap. A problem can often occur when the toddler reaches a stage where he no longer needs two naps a day, but becomes very over-tired when he is only having one. This over-tiredness can result in problems in settling in the evening. If this is not dealt with properly, a baby who has always slept well can, when he enters toddlerhood, suddenly start waking up in the night.

Another problem that often arises for parents with babies who have always slept well is that when they enter toddlerhood they suddenly start standing up in the cot or trying to climb out. A close eye should be kept on the amount of sleep that a toddler is having during the day at this stage, if night-time wakings are to be avoided or existing problems resolved.

What to aim for

Between 12 and 18 months the amount of day-time sleep is reduced to between 1½ to two hours a day. The majority of toddlers who are sleeping well at night will, between 12 and 15 months of age, cut back their morning sleep to 15–20 minutes a day, and by 18 months have cut it out altogether, having a two-hour nap in the middle of the day. If your toddler is cutting back on his lunchtime nap, waking up earlier in the morning or not settling well in the evening, he is probably ready to cut down on his day-time sleep. If he is having more than 20 minutes in the morning, it is advisable to cut right back on this first nap of the day, to no more than 15–20 minutes. If he is only having 15–20 minutes, it may be worthwhile trying to get him to go through the morning without a nap. If you allow him to nap longer in the morning or fail to eliminate the morning nap when he is ready to reduce the amount of sleep he needs, he will more than likely start to resist going to bed in the evening, waking earlier in the morning or waking in the middle of the night.

Between 12 and 24 months a typical day would look similar to the following, although adaptations will have to sometimes be made with sleep, depending on social activities.

7/7.30am	awake, milk feed followed by breakfast
9.30am	short nap of 15/30 minutes, gradually eliminated by 18 months
11.45/noon	lunch
12.30/1pm	nap-time – no more than two hours
5pm	tea
5.45pm	bath and bedtime routine
7/7.30pm	asleep

The bedtime routine

If you have established a later bedtime of 7.30 or 8pm, you may find that once your toddler stops having his early morning nap he gets very over-tired and needs to go to bed slightly earlier. Over-tiredness can be a real problem during the second year as it during this stage that the toddler begins to learn many new skills, which can leave him both physically and mentally exhausted. It is very important to start winding things down after tea and to maintain a very calm quiet bedtime routine.

At this age toddlers who have just learned to walk can become very excitable in the early evening, wanting to run around playing chase or hide and seek. What starts out to be a fun game nearly always ends in tears as the toddler gets a second wind and refuses to calm down.

Common problems

- Night-time feeding
- Early morning waking
- Refusal to go to bed
- Getting out of the cot or bed
- Poor day-time sleep

Night-time feeding

If your toddler is still needing to be fed to sleep and wakes several times a night refusing to settle back to sleep without a feed, it is important that you look very closely at his day-time feeding before embarking on any form of sleep-training. All too often parents attempt to sleep-train toddlers with disastrous results. They are told that their toddler does not need to feed in the night and that using controlled crying will quickly resolve the problem. After two or three nights of the toddler screaming for hours, these parents usually abandon controlled crying, claiming that it did not work for them. I believe the advice that toddlers don't need feeding in the night should be replaced with 'shouldn't need feeding in the night'. The reason that sleep-training has not worked for these toddlers is that they are genuinely hungry at some of the wakings in the night. This is a result of demand feeding in the very early days. Because the milk feeds were never structured properly, the baby was never given the opportunity to increase his day-time feeding. A vicious cycle soon evolves of the baby needing to make up his daily nutritional needs in the night because he did not feed well in the day, along with the wrong association of falling asleep on the breast or bottle, which leads to a very serious problem.

Because this is more than just an association problem, it is important that steps are taken to improve the day-time feeding before sleep-training is used to eliminate the association problem.

Case Study – Rachel, aged 17 months

Problem: waking up six to seven times a night

Cause: associating falling asleep with breast feeding

Kate contacted me when she was four months pregnant with her second baby. She was very concerned about her elder daughter Rachel, who was then 17 months old and still waking up several times a night and refusing to settle back to sleep unless she was given a quick breast feed. Rachel had no set routine during the day, and rarely fell asleep much before 10pm in the evening. The only way Kate could get her to sleep and into her cot at night was to lie on her bed and feed Rachel to sleep, then transfering her to her cot once she was in a deep sleep. This could often take up to two hours. If Rachel was put into the cot before she was in a very deep sleep, she would wake up within five or ten minutes and Kate would have to start the whole procedure again. Once asleep, she rarely went longer than an hour before she would wake up screaming and refuse to settle until she was put to the breast again. Sometimes Kate could settle her back asleep in the cot again within 10 minutes, but other times it would take up to an hour.

Kate was totally exhausted and worried sick about how she was going to cope when the new baby came along if Rachel was still waking several times in the night and needing to be breast fed-back to sleep. She had, on two different occasions, tried controlled crying. On the first occasion Rachel cried non-stop for three hours, and on the second occasion she cried for nearly an hour, went back to sleep for 40 minutes then cried for a further hour. Kate had become so stressed that she ended up feeding Rachel back to sleep on both occasions. She was desperate to wean Rachel from the breast and establish a routine before the new baby arrived, but felt that she couldn't cope with hours of crying again.

I explained that when a toddler has learned to wrong sleep associations over such a long period of time, it is very difficult to resolve the problem without some amount of crying. But I was sure that, like many toddlers who were still milk feeding in the night, Rachel was probably not eating enough during the day because she was having too much milk at night. Kate admitted that Rachel had never been very keen on her solids even as a young baby, and now her diet was even more limited.

Her breakfast usually consisted of a small fromage frais and one finger of toast, and lunch was normally made up of something like baked beans and mashed potatoes or alpha bites with ketchup, again followed by one or two small pots of fromage frais. At tea-time she might take some pasta with a cheesy sauce or oven chips, but at lunchtime never more than a couple of tablespoonfuls.

Rachel's day-time sleep was very erratic and she never slept more than 30 minutes at a time, and again this was only after she had been put to the breast. I explained to Kate that feeding Rachel to sleep had not only created the wrong sleep associations but was also affecting her appetite for solids. A vicious circle had emerged in which she was not only dependent on feeding to get to sleep, but she was also genuinely hungry in the night because she had not eaten enough solids during the day, and that was the reason that controlled crying would be very difficult to implement.

I advised Kate that we should try to improve Rachel's intake of solids before we attempted sleep-training at night. I was also concerned that Rachel ate so little protein, which is a very important food source for toddlers. I suggested to Kate that we should try to cut down on Rachel's breast milk intake during the day, so that her intake of solids increased, enabling us to decrease the need for milk in the night. On the first day of the plan I advised Kate to express most of the milk from her breasts at around 10.30am in the morning. Because Rachel always woke around 6am, she was usually very tired by 11am and Kate would give her a breast feed then to settle her to sleep. The sleep rarely lasted more than 30 minutes and when Rachel woke up at around 11.30am Kate would normally give her a biscuit or breadstick to get her through to lunch, which was usually around 12.30pm. I believe that the combination of the milk feed and the biscuit was taking the edge off Rachel's appetite.

This proved to be true, because after having a very small breast feed and no biscuit on the first day, Rachel was hungry for lunch at 12 noon. She ate nearly double what she normally did, and when she was ready for her next short nap, which usually came at around 3.30pm, she only needed to feed from one breast before she fell asleep. She then woke up as usual after 30 minutes. Instead of giving her the usual beaker of juice and a biscuit, I suggested that Kate give her only water and a small piece of fruit. Rachel was none too happy and had a tantrum. But Kate didn't give in. She distracted her, then took her to the park so that she would not keep going to the kitchen cupboard looking for the biscuit box.

That evening I told Kate that Rachel should be given most of her solids before the beaker of juice was offered, and that the juice should be diluted slightly. Because Rachel rarely ate fruit, Kate had been offering her full strength juice to replace the vitamins Rachel was missing out on. But I felt that excessive amounts of juice at the wrong times were also affecting Rachel's appetite and that we should gradually dilute the juice so that her vitamin intake eventually consisted of fruit and vegetables earlier in the day. I felt that Kate could be more relaxed about tea and allow Rachel to have a couple of biscuits, but advised her to choose healthier ones as opposed to those with lots of chocolate and additives in them. After the tea, at around 6pm, Rachel would normally have another breast feed and fall asleep on the sofa for a short nap. I advised Kate to feed Rachel from the same breast that she had fed on at 3.30pm so that she got enough milk to get to sleep, but not too much to put her off a really good feed prior to bedtime.

Rachel would normally have a bath around 8pm then be brought back downstairs for a story and a cuddle with Daddy, before being taken back upstairs for her bedtime feed. More often than not Rachel would get a second wind and would start running around playing with her toys and be very difficult to calm down once she was taken back upstairs. I advised Kate not to bring Rachel back downstairs but after the bath to spend between 15 and 20 minutes reading to her before settling her with her breast feed.

Kate was very full on the breast that she had not fed Rachel from at 11am and she offered her that first. Rachel fed very well and fell asleep within 30 minutes; however, when Kate tried to transfer her to her cot she quickly woke up. As advised, Kate lay down on the bed with her again. Although this was not ideal, I felt it was better than taking Rachel back downstairs and allowing her to run around and become very over-tired. Rachel did get very irritable that evening and it took a lot of cuddling and feeding on and off before she settled in her cot around 10pm.

However, once asleep she actually slept past her normal first waking time of between 12am and 1am, and because Kate's breasts had gone longer between feeds they were again quite full. Rachel fed well from one breast at 2am and settled back to sleep until 5am. She then took a very full breast but refused to settle back to sleep. When Kate phoned me that morning, I advised her not to offer Rachel a further breast feed until after her lunch, as we should count the feed at 5am as her breakfast feed. That day Rachel ate even more at lunchtime than the previous day and fell asleep after only a few minutes on the breast.

She also slept nearly 50 minutes that lunchtime, which was unsual for her. So I advised Kate to try and push Rachel through the rest of the day without any sleep – which also meant that we could cut out the mid-afternoon breast feed. Kate was worried that Rachel would not be getting enough milk that day, but I explained that we must calculate her milk intake over 24-hour period, not just what she had during the day. From midnight that day she had already had two good feeds, so I felt confident that by the time she had one or two more feeds that day she would have had more than her daily requirement. I explained to Kate that Rachel's sleeping problem was not just being caused by the wrong sleep association but that she was genuinely hungry. I explained again the importance of cutting down her milk during the day so that she would eat more solids and that once she was eating more solids during the day she would not want to drink so much milk during the night. Once we had eliminated the night feeds we could then give her milk feeds at the regular times during the day.

Although Rachel got a bit grumpy that afternoon, Kate didn't resort to breast feeding her but she did have to bring her teatime forward to 4.40pm. Rachel had a really good tea, but was getting very tired by 5.30pm, so Kate started the bath early and was feeding Rachel by 6pm. Again she kept her upstairs in the dark and lay on the bed with her, feeding her on and off, until she fell asleep at 9pm. She woke again at midnight, but this time she did not seem very hungry and, although it took nearly an hour, Kate persisted in settling her by cuddling and rocking her. She then slept soundly until 2am, when she took a good feed from both breasts and went back to sleep until nearer 6.30am.

I felt that this next day was the window of opportunity and we could start to use sleep-training, confident that Rachel would not be genuinely hungry in the night. She fed from the breast at 6.30am, then had lunch at 11.30am before settling to sleep with a breast feed at 12.15pm. She slept for nearly an hour and again Kate got her through the afternoon without a breast feed. That evening I suggested that, provided Rachel had a good breast feed, Kate should attempt to put her in her cot when she was getting sleepy but not fully asleep. She should then use the checking method every five minutes for the first half hour, increasing it to 10 minutes the next half hour. It took nearly an hour and a half of crying on and off, with Kate checking Rachel every 15 minutes, before Rachel eventually fell asleep. She did, however, sleep until nearly 3am, when she fed from one breast, settled well, and slept until nearly 7am, when she woke and fed again well from one breast. We followed the same pattern as the previous day and that evening Rachel settled within 25 minutes and slept until 3.30am, when she fed well and settled back to sleep until 7am.

On the third night Rachel settled to sleep within 10 minutes, and both Kate and I felt that she had eaten well enough during the day that when she woke she could be offered cool boiled water instead of a breast feed. She slept until 3.30am and when Kate tried to settle her back with water she got very upset; however, Kate decided that she was confident enough to do controlled crying at this time as Rachel had proven that she could settle herself to sleep in the evening. The crying lasted nearly 45 minutes, with Kate checking Rachel every 15–20 minutes. By the fifth night Rachel was sleeping through from 7pm to 6/7am, and crying for no more than 10 minutes in the evening and 10–15 minutes in the night. By the end of the week she was actually settling herself to sleep in the evening and back to sleep in the night when she awoke without crying at all.

Kate realised that the midday nap was still a problem, as Rachel was still being fed to sleep then. I advised her to start to offer Rachel well-diluted juice or water after her lunch so that she could gradually cut down the length of time she was put on the breast to settle to sleep. Within a week Kate had the feed down to three minutes and she then decided to do controlled crying at lunchtime. Rachel cried for between 15 and 20 minutes the first day, 10 the second and only a few seconds the third day.

Kate continued to breast feed for a further three weeks before gradually weaning Rachel from the breast to a beaker.

Case Study – Lauren, aged 22 months

Problem: milk feeding in the night

Cause: association and hunger

Lauren had been breast-fed on demand for the first eight months of her life and would only ever fall asleep while feeding on the breast. She would settle in her cot at 7.30pm and would then sleep well until 10pm, when she would have another breast feed. She would wake a further two or three times in the night and would always have to be settled back to sleep with a breast feed.

Beth, her mother, was happy to continue feeding as often as Lauren demanded in the night because she was confident that once Lauren was weaned she would gradually cut out night feeds altogether. Lauren was introduced to solids at five months, but she was a very reluctant and fussy feeder and by the time she reached six months she was eating no more than a couple of teaspoonfuls of solids at each meal. Her weight gain also began to drop rapidly and, although she was still feeding from the breast several times a day and two or three times a night, Beth felt that her breast milk supply was diminishing and was not confident that Lauren was getting enough milk.

At eight months she gradually weaned Lauren on to formula. Lauren still needed to be fed to sleep but once asleep she would sleep longer between feeds. After her 7pm feed she started to sleep through until midnight, when she would take 180–210ml (6–7oz) and settle back to sleep until around 5am, when she would have a further 150–180ml (5–6oz) of milk. Sometimes she would settle back to sleep but more often than not she would be ready to start the day. Beth would offer Lauren breakfast around 7am, but she would rarely eat more than a few teaspoonfuls.

Because of the early waking, Lauren would get very tired by 9/9.30am in the morning. She would then have to be given a further 150–180ml (5-6oz) feed to get her to sleep. Once asleep she would normally sleep for 1–1½ hours. When she woke at 11am she was given a small drink of juice so that she could get through to 12 noon, when she was offered lunch. Some days she would eat better than others, but on the whole lunchtimes were a nightmare and it was only with much singing and distraction that Beth would manage to get Lauren to take a few spoonfuls of food.

Lauren would become tired around 3pm, when she would have a further milk feed of about 150ml (5oz) before falling asleep for about 40 minutes. She was given tea at around 4.30pm and again it was always a battle, with very little solid food being eaten. At 7pm she would take a good formula feed of around 240ml (8oz) before falling asleep in her mother's arms. Beth continued to feed Lauren formula milk in the night until she was nearly 20 months but she was getting increasingly worried about Lauren's poor eating and exhausted by still having to get up and feed her twice in the night.

On the advice of a friend, Beth bought the book *Solve Your Child's Sleeping Problems* by Richard Ferber. After reading the book from cover to cover she began to understand how she had created the wrong sleep association by always feeding Lauren to sleep. She learnt that Lauren's excessive night-time feeding was contributing to her poor eating habits during the day. Following the guidelines in the book, she started to gradually dilute the first feed of the night, which came at around midnight. Within a week she was managing to settle Lauren back to sleep at midnight with a small drink of water. However, she started to wake for the second feed of the night much earlier than 5am, normally at 3am. Beth persevered and gradually diluted the second feed. Getting rid of the second feed of the night did not prove as easy as getting rid of the first. Once it reached the stage where the feed was made up of 150ml (5oz) of water and 2 scoops of milk powder, Lauren would rarely settle back to sleep for more than 30 or 40 minutes at a time. Because they had read that babies over six months do not need to milk feed in the night, they decided to do controlled crying. After four nights of Lauren screaming on and off between 3am and 6am, they rang me asking for help.

I advised them to go back to feeding Lauren a full-strength feed in the night so that she settled back to sleep quickly. I suggested that for several days we should dilute the day-time feeds so that Lauren's solid intake increased. Once we had seen a significant increase in her solids we could then start to dilute the middle of the night feed. I explained to Beth that Lauren genuinely needed the milk feed in the night because her day-time solid intake was so poor and that controlled crying would not be successful because her need for milk was genuine.

Over the next few days we decreased the strength of the 9am feed by one scoop each day until she was taking 150ml (5oz) of water with only one scoop of powder. We then saw a dramatic improvement in the amount of solids that Lauren ate at lunchtime, which had the knock-on effect of her not drinking so much milk at 3pm and eating more solids at teatime. Because Lauren had increased her teatime solids, the amount she drank at 7pm dropped by a couple of ounces but she actually started to sleep until nearer 4.30. She then took a full 210ml (7oz) and would sleep until nearer 6.30am. I advised Beth to count the 4.30am milk feed as Lauren's breakfast feed and to offer her solids before offering her a top-up of milk after the solids.

The following day, she slept until 6am and I suggested that Beth try to push her through the morning without a nap, thus eliminating the need to give the diluted feed at 9am. At 11am she started to get very tired and hungry, so I advised Beth to give her an early lunch so that over-tiredness did not affect her appetite. She ate a very good lunch and then took a feed of 150ml (5oz) of full strength milk before falling asleep at around 11.45am. She then slept nearly an hour and a half and Beth managed to get her through the afternoon without another nap, which meant that she did not need to be offered a further milk feed until bedtime. Beth offered her a small drink of well-diluted juice at around 3.30pm that afternoon, and Lauren was happy to wait until 5pm for her tea. She ate an excellent tea and drank nearly 210ml (7oz) when she went to bed that night.

The next three days followed the same pattern, with Lauren taking a 210ml (7oz) milk feed at 4.30am followed by a top-up of 90ml (3oz) after breakfast and 150ml (5oz) at

11.45am, followed by 210ml (7oz) at bedtime. Lauren's daily intake was around 660ml (22oz) of milk a day, which was more than the recommended amount of 360ml (12oz) a day, plus she was eating three good solid meals a day. I felt that we could now start to gradually dilute the 3.40am feed without worrying that Lauren could possibly be genuinely hungry. Within six nights we had Lauren taking a diluted feed of 180ml (6oz) water to one scoop of milk powder and settling back to sleep. She would wake and take a full strength feed of 180ml (6oz) of formula. I advised Beth that Lauren was now having all her nutritional needs met during the day and that she could now attempt sleep-training with the confidence that within three or four nights Lauren would have learned to settle herself to sleep.

That night Lauren was put in her cot at 7pm, sleepy but awake, and Beth used the checking method over the next hour until she had fallen asleep. The following night I advised Beth to increase the checking time to every 10 minutes. Lauren fell asleep within 20 minutes on the second night, and on the third night Beth did not even have to go in to check her, as she had fallen asleep within five minutes.

Having sorted out the evening settling, Beth then went on to use the controlled crying method when Lauren woke at 4.30am. After four nights of gradually increasing the intervals between checking Lauren in the night, Beth felt confident on the fifth night that Lauren was capable of getting herself back to sleep and only went in if Lauren sounded in distress. Lauren actually only cried on and off for 20 minutes before going back to sleep until nearer 7am. Now that Lauren was going down awake and sleeping soundly from 7.30pm to 7am, Beth decided to tackle the lunchtime nap. She settled Lauren in her cot awake and decided to wait 20 minutes before checking her. Lauren cried for eight minutes before settling herself to sleep. Lauren continues to sleep well at night and eat well and enjoy her solids.

Early-morning waking

During the second year, early waking can sometimes become a problem if the first nap of the day is not structured properly. If the toddler continues to have a longer morning nap once his sleep requirements are reduced, he will usually start to cut back on his midday nap. This usually has the knock-on effect of him becoming tired earlier in the evening and possibly falling into a very deep sleep much quicker – usually between 6.30pm and 7pm. Over a period of time the earlier bedtime will result in him starting to wake up earlier and earlier. If this problem is to be avoided, it is important to gradually start cutting back the first nap of the day, so that he is only having around 15 minutes by the time he reaches 15–18 months, when it can usually be dropped altogether.

A similar problem can occur when parents fail to keep pushing the morning nap forward to between 9.30am and 9.45am. A baby who is sleeping to 7am should, as his need for sleep is reduced, manage to go longer than two hours before needing his morning nap. Parents who continue to put their toddler down at 9am, will normally have to continue to put him down for the lunchtime nap at 12 noon. During the second year the toddler becomes much more physically active and is prone to over-tiredness late in the day, again resulting in him becoming tired earlier in the evening. If the first nap of the day is pushed forward, then the second nap can be pushed from 12.30pm to 1pm, avoiding the problem of early evening over-tiredness.

Another major cause of early-morning waking, particularly between 18 and 24 months is that parents have established the longer nap of the day in the morning. During the first year this does not usually present a real problem, but near the end of the second year, when the toddler is ready to cut down on his sleep, it will usually be the shortest nap of the day. When the shortest nap of the day is the afternoon nap, it will result in a very over-tired toddler who struggles to get through the day without a second nap. If your child is sleeping longer in the morning, with only a 45-minute nap or less in the afternoon, it is advisable to gradually reduce the morning nap by 10 minutes every two or three days until he is only having 15–20 minutes in the morning. This should hopefully enable you to establish a longer nap of 1–1½ hours at around 12.30 to 1pm.

Refusal to go to bed

Over-tiredness is one of the main causes of bedtime battles during the second year. As the toddler learns many new skills, in particular walking and talking, his confidence increases and he becomes much more assertive. His natural desire to take more responsibility and control of his own actions will often lead to him devising his own bedtime routine. While it is important to avoid confrontation and upset at bedtime, it is essential that you remain consistent with the routine and that it does not get increasingly longer, which will result in him getting a second wind and fighting sleep.

The lack of structure with the morning nap can, again, be the cause of problems at bedtime. A child who continues to have a 45-minute nap or longer in the morning followed by a two-hour nap at midday or later will, when his sleep requirements reduce, start to fight sleep at his normal bedtime.

Getting out of the cot or bed

Babies who are put in a sleeping bag during the first year rarely attempt to get out of the cot, as it is physically impossible for them to straddle their legs. I always advise parents to keep their toddler in a cot until they are nearly three years of age so that the problem of getting out of bed does not become an issue. However, occasionally I have known a very agile toddler to hurl himself out of the cot. When this happens it is safer to put him in a bed and accept that you will have to go through a short spell of very firmly marching him back to his own bed. This should be done very quickly and quietly without conversation. It may need to be done up to 20 times a night for several nights, but if you persevere he will eventually get fed up and take the hint that it is not worth his while getting out of bed.

Case Study – Joseph, aged 18 months

Problem: refusing to sleep alone

Cause: getting out of the cot

Joseph had always slept well until the age of 15 months, when one night his parents were suddenly woken by a very loud thud and hysterical secreaming. They rushed straight to Joseph's room to find him lying on the floor shaking and crying uncontrollably. Somehow, despite the room being very dark, Joseph had woken up and managed to get out of his sleeping bag and attempted to climb out of the cot. It was obvious from the way he was holding his right arm when they tried to pick him up that he was in a lot of pain. The doctor was called and fortunately there were no broken bones, but they were told that Joseph would probably be badly bruised and in some pain for a few days. The doctor gave Joseph some medication for the pain and to help calm him down.

Joseph spent the remainder of the night in his parents' bed. The following day, on the advice of the doctor, his parents removed the cot from his room and replaced it with a single bed from their spare room. When they tried to settle him for his lunchtime nap he became hysterical the minute they took him into his room, and clung to his mother, Jackie, becoming even more hysterical when she tried to settle him down in the new bed.

Jackie realised that the painful fall had left Joseph with a bad association, so that lunchtime she stayed with him in his room, sitting on a chair next to the bed so that she could keep reassuring him that everything was okay. It took nearly half an hour for Joseph to fall asleep, and even then it was only for 40 minutes, a much shorter nap than he normally had.

Jackie tried to settle him back to sleep but he got so

upset that after 20 minutes she gave up and took him downstairs. That evening a similar pattern occurred when Jackie tried to settle him to sleep. He got very upset when put in his bed, and when he did eventually fall asleep it was a very disturbed sleep, with him crying out every 20 minutes or so.

Eventually Joseph went into a deep sleep at around 10pm in the evening. His parents thought all was well until Joseph tried to get into their bed at around 1am. They realised that a problem could very quickly evolve if they allowed him into their bed and they took him back to his own bed immediately. Mark, his father, sat next to the bed quietly reassuring Joseph that everything was all right. Joseph eventually fell asleep around 1.45am and Mark returned to his own room, only to be woken by Joseph trying yet again to get into the bed at around 3am. This time Jackie took him back and resettled him, which took another 40 minutes. Joseph slept well until 6am, when he again appeared at his parents' bedside. Both Mark and Jackie were so exhausted that they decided that being so near the morning it would do no harm to allow Joseph in bed for an hour so that they could all catch up on some sleep.

Over the next eight nights a similar pattern occurred, with Joseph taking a long time to settle and waking up several times a night trying to get into his parents' bed. Although they did try to settle him back in his own bed each time, by the ninth night they were so exhausted that they gave in and allowed him to sleep in their bed. After two more weeks of Joseph taking a long time to settle at night and then eventually, around 1 am, getting into his parents' bed, all three were becoming more and more exhausted by bed sharing and Mark would end up getting into Joseph's bed when he got into their bed.

By the time Joseph reached 18 months Mark and Jackie were beginnning to disagree about the sleeping arrangements and how best to deal with the problem. Mark was feeling resentful that when he got home in the evening he hardly saw Jackie as one of them always had to spend at least an hour settling Joseph to sleep, and often he would sleep for only 40 minutes before waking up, getting out of bed and trying to get downstairs.

When he did eventually get to sleep it was rarely more than a couple of hours before he would come downstairs or try to get into his parents' bed. Jackie and Mark, realising that the problem was affecting their marriage, rang me for advice on how best to try and resolve the problem. The first thing I advised them to do was buy a very strong high stair-gate to put across the bedroom door. I suggested that they fit the gate low enough to the floor that Joseph could not crawl under it, but high up enough that he could not climb over the top. From the description of the single bed, it appeared to be far too high for such a young toddler, especially one who had fallen out of his cot, so I suggested that they remove the base from the single bed and put the mattress on the floor.

Because Joseph had got so used to sleeping in his parents' room, I advised that we should spend a week using the gradual withdrawal method to get him used to his own room before attempting any tougher form of sleep-training. On the first night Jackie and Mark settled Joseph in his bed as they had been doing, sitting with him until he went to sleep. When he woke up the next time and tried to get out of the room, he couldn't because of the stair-gate. This allowed Mark to get to him before he got out of the room and, as we had agreed, Mark sat with him by the bed until he fell asleep again.

We agreed that for the next three nights Mark and Jackie would sleep in the room with Joseph so that he got used to sleeping back in his own room. It also meant that they could get him straight back into bed the minute he got out. They followed the same pattern until Friday night, when we agreed that they would start to implement the withdrawal method when settling Joseph to bed that evening. They would sit with him for 10 minutes, then leave the room for two minutes, but calling out to reassure him that they would be back in a minute. After 30 minutes they felt that they could increase the time they were out of the room by a further minute to three minutes.

Joseph eventually fell asleep after half an hour, and when he woke the next time they followed the same procedure but increased the time they were out of the room to four minutes. He woke a further two times in the night and each time they followed the same procedure.

We followed this routine for a further week and although things improved slightly Mark and Jackie were getting absolutely exhausted and worried that they were losing their resolve, so they decided that they were prepared to attempt controlled crying.

The following night they settled Joseph in his bed but instead of sitting by the bedside they left the room. Of course Joseph got out of bed immediately. He screamed and shouted, rattling the gate and trying to climb out. Mark, who was in the room next door, would go to the gate every two minutes and tell Joseph that it was night-time and he must go back to bed. After an hour of screaming and rattling the gate, Joseph eventually crawled into bed and fell asleep. He awoke twice more that night and Mark carried out the same procedure each time. On both occasions it took nearly an hour for Joseph to get to sleep. On the second night of controlled crying we increased the checking time to every three minutes and this time Joseph fell asleep after 25 minutes. He only woke once more that night and Mark decreased the checking time to every five minutes. He settled within 30 minutes.

On the third night Joseph did not get out of bed and the

crying was not as intense, so Mark used a checking of every five minutes. Joseph settled within 20 minutes and actually slept right through the night. Although they did hear him stir a few times he did not cry out. On the fourth night Mark waited 10 minutes before going to check Joseph, and Joseph actually settled with 15 minutes. He stirred again several times in the night but did not call out.

On the fifth night Mark decided to wait 15 minutes before checking Joseph, but Joseph actually fell asleep after eight minutes of mild protesting. It was a further week before Joseph fell asleep without protesting, but the crying got less intense each night and lasted for shorter periods of time.

Poor day-time naps

If proper day-time naps have been established during the first year, with some of the naps always being in the cot, a problem should not really occur. However, during the first year babies are so transportable that many parents get into the habit of allowing all the naps to be taken in the car or the buggy. The problem with this is that as the child becomes bigger and more physically active, it becomes more difficult to induce a nap for any length of time. This usually results in a toddler who will catnap two or three times a day for no longer than 15–20 minutes at a time. This results in a very fretful irritable toddler who is much more prone to tantrums than a toddler who is having one longer stretch of sound sleep during the day.

During the second year, day-time naps can often go wrong for even the best of sleepers. If your toddler always slept well at nap-times during his first year but suddenly starts to resist sleep during the second year, the cause is probably sleeping too long at the wrong nap-time. For example a baby who sleeps until nearly 7am in the morning should during the second year have his first nap of the day pushed forward to 9.30am and gradually cut down so that he continues to sleep well at the midday nap.

By the time a toddler reaches 18 months he should have cut out the morning nap altogether. If you allow your toddler to continue with even a short nap in the morning at this stage, it is possible that he will cut right back at the midday nap.

Another reason why day-time sleep goes wrong during the second year is that a toddler reaches a stage where he no longer needs two naps but cannot manage to get through until after lunch for his midday nap. When this happens you may have to bring forward the time he has his lunch so that he can be in bed somewhere between 12.15pm and 12.30pm. Once he shows signs of not getting so tired in the late morning, you can push the lunchtime nap later again.

It is also important to stick to the same rituals for the day-time naps and not allow the settling procedure to extend. Toddlers of this age often start using delaying tactics at sleep-times and attempt to create their own rituals. It is important to stay consistent and persistent, so that your toddler realises that, even if he is not quite ready to sleep, once he is in his bedroom it is quiet time.

6

The Older Child – Two to Three Years

What to expect

At this stage the amount of sleep required will normally have dropped to an average of 12–13 hours a day. The amount of sleep required at night is usually slightly reduced and the majority of children will cut right back on their day-time sleep. The length of time they nap for can vary from day to day; sometimes they may sleep between one to two hours, other days they may only sleep one hour. By the time most children reach three years of age they have cut out the middle of the day nap altogether. However, many parents encourage their child to have a short period of quiet time in their bedroom.

What to aim for

It is important to monitor your child's day-time sleep very closely during this stage, to ensure that, as the amount of sleep he needs decreases, the sleep he cuts back on is during the day and not at night. In my experience a sound night's sleep is essential if the child is to cope with the high demand on his energy levels during the day. Keeping a close eye on his day-time activities to ensure that he does not burn out at this stage is vital. Burn-out can happen when a toddler becomes exhausted with activities and play dates and doesn't have enough quiet time or rest to recharge his batteries. Maintaining a calm consistent bedtime routine is also a key factor in maintaining good-quality sleep at night.

Between two and three years of age a typical day would look something like the following:

7/7.30am	awake, drink and breakfast
9/10am	play school or social activity
12/12.30pm	lunch
1pm	short nap/rest time
2pm	play school or social activity
5pm	tea
6pm	bath/bed routine – may need to start earlier on the arrival of a new baby
7/7.30pm	settled in bed no later than 7.30pm

The bedtime routine

Things can get very fraught at bedtime during this stage as it often coincides with the arrival of a new baby. Getting a tired child and a young baby into bed happily by 7pm takes a great deal of energy and manipulative skill if things are not to end up like a battle ground. It is still very important to keep the bedtime routine calm and quiet. Children of this age do like to have a little play after their tea, but try to avoid noisy games or getting the child over-excited. Do not let your toddler watch a video before the bath. A video or a story after the bath can be used as an incentive to encourage your child to undress himself and get into the bath quickly. A child of this age is capable of taking off most of his own clothes at bath-time, and should be encouraged to do so, especially if there is young baby to settle as well or one is on the way. It is important to allow more time before the bath, as things will obviously take much longer than when you were undressing him.

It is important to be consistent with the ritual after the bath and not allow your child to keep devising new rituals. Allow no more than 30 minutes between the time your child gets out of the bath and the time he goes to bed, as more time often results in a child getting a second wind and being very difficult to settle. A child of this age who deliberately dawdles when getting dressed needs to learn that this will result in a shorter story time. It is important to stick to the same time for settling him in his cot or bed, even if he appears to be anxious about being left alone. If he is very fretful you can use the checking method to reassure him that you are close at hand. But do not allow him to lead you into lengthy conversations when you go in to check him. Leaving a small night-light on and allowing him to listen to a nursery rhyme or story tape, along with the checking method, is a great way of teaching him to get off to sleep by himself.

Common Problems

- Bedtime Difficulties
- Overtiredness
- Nightmares and night terrors
- Arrival of a new baby
- The big bed

Bedtime difficulties

A child who has always settled easily at bedtime will often start resisting sleep and refusing to fall asleep alone, protesting loudly when his parents leave the room. He suddenly develops night-time fears and anxieties. Fear of the dark and talk of monsters are very common at this stage, and should be dealt with sensitively but firmly. In my experience a child who has always settled well but suddenly becomes dependent on either of his parents being in the room while he falls asleep will very quickly learn the wrong sleep associations. He will more than likely start to wake up in the night and expect one of his parents to be there until he goes back to sleep.

The first sign of this problem is that the child begins to use delaying tactics at bedtime, asking for yet another story or drink, or to use the potty. How you deal with this problem depends on whether your child is sleeping in a cot or a bed. If your child is still in a cot you can use the checking method to help him learn to get to sleep. This way he will not feel that you are totally abandoning him and will also realise that you are not going to keep giving in to his constant demands. If he has already moved to a bed, you will probably find that he will keep getting out of bed if left alone, so using the gradual withdrawal method will probably work better. At this age I would not insist that a child sleeps in total darkness if he asks for the light to be left on. I would agree to leave a small plug-in night socket light on until the child goes to sleep, on the understanding that he lies quietly in bed. Between two and three years the majority of children will have cut down dramatically on their day-time sleep, and by the time they reach three years of age, most will have given up the day-time nap altogether. If your child is becoming more difficult to settle at night, it is important to make sure that the reason he is not settling at bedtime is that he is having too much sleep during the day.

Over-tiredness

Not getting enough sleep during the day can also cause problems at bedtime, particularly with a child under 30 months who has dropped his day-time sleep. During this stage day-time activities have usually increased, demanding more of the child's mental and physical energy. Even the most easy-going of children can start to play up at bedtime, and over-tiredness is one of the main reasons why a child who used to settle easily at bedtime becomes more difficult. A child you used to settle happily at around 7.30pm may need the bedtime routine brought forward so that he is bed by 7pm, particularly if he has not had a nap that day.

Case Study – Samantha, aged 28 months

Problem: difficulty in settling to sleep

Cause: over-tiredness and fear of the dark

Samantha had never had a set bedtime routine and was never put in her own cot until her parents went to bed at around 11pm. She would often fall asleep during the early part of the evening on the living room sofa, but never for more than 30–40 minutes at a time. She would then wake up at least twice in the night and have to be resettled back to sleep by her mother, usually by being cuddled or being given a drink of juice, and sometimes both. She would awaken at around 6am in the morning, ready to start the day. During the day she would have a couple of short naps usually lasting between 20 and 40 minutes, either in the car or in her buggy. She never went in her cot during the day, and her sleep in total over a 24-hour day was around nine hours, which is considerably less than a child of her age usually needs. When Samantha was just over two years old, her mother went back to work part-time, which meant that Samantha started to go to nursery three days a week. She was dropped off at 8am in the morning by her father then picked up in the evening by her mother at around 5pm.

Because Samantha had only ever been used to sleeping in the car or her buggy during the day, she would not settle down for a nap alongside the other children after lunch. By the time her mother picked her up in the evening she was totally exhausted and usually fell asleep during the 20-minute car journey home. Her mother, now working three days a week as a carer in a residential home for the elderly, was also exhausted at the end of her nine-hour shift. She began to find it increasingly difficult to cope with Samantha's late bedtime and middle of the night wakings and decided that a earlier bedtime for both her and Samantha was necessary if she was going to be able to cope with her demanding job. She believed that Samantha was a child who needed less sleep than the average recommendation and aimed to bring her bedtime forward to around 9pm. She started a bath and bedtime routine at around 8pm, in the hope that she could settle her in the cot by 9pm.

Unfortunately, because Samantha had only ever gone into her cot when she was absolutely exhausted, establishing an earlier bedtime and a routine proved much more difficult than her mother had imagined.

Samantha would scream and scream the minute she was put in her cot. Often she would get so hysterical that she would throw up. She continued to wake up in the night but started to take longer and longer to settle back to sleep, and even then would only do so if the bedroom door was left open and her light full on. After two weeks of trying to establish a routine using the controlled crying method, things had got worse. Her mother rang me desperate for advice on how to establish a bedtime routine and improve on Samantha's night-time sleep.

I explained to her that Samantha's main problems were that she had learned all the wrong sleep associations. In addition she suffered from serious over-tiredness, fighting sleep and being able to fall asleep only when absolutely exhausted. There was also the fact that she was used to sleeping on and off during the earlier part of her night in the sitting room, where there was always a light on. To expect her suddenly to settle in her cot by herself in a dark room was unrealistic at an age when even the best of sleepers start to experience all sorts of fears and anxieties. I advised that with Samantha the best way to resolve the problem would be to use the gradual withdrawal method. It could take several weeks to establish but in Samantha's case it would be probably more effective than controlled crying.

I advised her mother to start Samantha's bedtime routine no later than 6pm and have her settled in her cot by 7pm. However, for the first few nights the light should be left low and she should stay in the room with her. I wanted to create the same atmosphere in her bedroom that she was used to in the sitting room during the early evening. Samantha could have toys in her cot and look at books, and listen to tapes on her cassette recorder. Her mother should potter around the room and sit in the chair reading a book, but everything should be kept very low-key, with talking kept to the minimum. When Samantha eventually fell asleep at around 11pm her mother could leave the room, and when she woke in the night her mother was to return, give her a quick drink and a cuddle to reassure her, but not talk at great length. She should remain in the room but sitting on the chair until Samantha fell back to sleep.

By the fifth night Samantha was adapting to her new evening routine and actually falling asleep much earlier, usually around 9.30pm. I advised her mother that she should now install an even dimmer night-light and limit the toys and books in the cot. She should also start to leave the room every 15 minutes for around one minute at a time, standing outside the door and reassuring Samantha that she would be back in a minute. The time should be extended by a further 30 seconds every 15 minutes until she reached a stage where she was leaving the room for five minutes every 15 minutes. The same procedure had to be followed in the night after she had been given a quick cuddle and a small drink. We continued this pattern for a further week, after which time I felt that Samantha was well used to the room, the bedtime routine and being in her cot from 7pm, and that we could try again the controlled crying method.

On the first night of controlled crying Samantha was settled in her cot with two of her favourite toys and with a very low voltage night-light. Her mother kissed her goodnight at 7pm and turned on her music tape. Samantha started to protest but her mother quickly left the room and waited 10 minutes before she returned. On her return she stayed in the room only one or two minutes and reassured Samantha that she was only next door and that it was night-time and everyone had to be very quiet at night-time. She would then leave the room and wait a further 15 minutes before returning and going through the same procedure. After about 50 minutes Samantha fell asleep. When she woke two hours later, her mother repeated the same procedure as before but after the first checking at 15 minutes she increased the time between visits to 20 minutes.

She continued the same procedure every night for over a week, but gradually increasing the time between visits and decreasing the amount of reassurance she gave Samantha. A following week of controlled crying got increasingly easier and some nights Samantha settled herself back before her mother was due to check her. By the end of the final week of sleep-training Samantha was settling easily in her cot with her music, usually falling asleep between 7.15pm and 7.30pm.

She would usually sleep soundly until 6/6.30am but would stay happily in her cot until 7am.

Nightmares

Although the majority of childcare experts say that nightmares are most common between the ages of three and six years, I personally believe that they can start much earlier, and when working as a maternity nurse often had to deal with children as young as two years old who were experiencing nightmares. Dr Richard Ferber says that children can experience dreams and nightmares from the second year of life, but at this age do not understand the difference between dreaming and reality. He says that nightmares are mainly a symptom of day-time emotional struggles. He believes that most nightmares do reflect emotional conflicts, but in most cases neither the nightmares nor the conflicts are 'abnormal'. Rather, the normal emotional struggles of growing up are at times significant enough to lead to occasional nightmares. Nightmares usually occur during an REM sleep cycle, often referred to as the light sleep cycle. If your child has always slept well and suddenly wakes up screaming during the second half of the night, he is probably having a bad dream and should be comforted and reassured immediately. Because a child of this age is still not able to grasp the difference between dreaming and reality, it is pointless trying to convince him that the monster doesn't exist. In my experience parents who do this only cause the child to become more upset. I have found the best approach is to follow the advice of Dr John Pearce and Dr Miriam Stoppard and work out a plan for how best to deal with the monster, i.e. making the monster fall into a hole or saying a magical spell to make it disappear.

Should your child wake up crying repeatedly over several weeks it is advisable to look at what is happening during the day to see if there is a particular reason for the bad dreams. Keeping a detailed diary of his day-time activities and details of the nightmare will often help pinpoint something or someone that could be causing him distress.

The following guidelines list the most common causes of frequent nightmares and how to deal with them:

- Bedtime stories and videos that involve violence or have a frightening story-line can cause some children to have nightmares. A child under three years of age is unlikely to understand the difference between fantasy and reality, and stories and videos should be monitored to ensure that they are suitable for your child's age. If you have an older child it may be necessary to stagger the bedtimes for a short while so that the younger one is not subjected to anything frightening. Even a story such as Little Red Riding Hood or The Three Little Pigs is enough to trigger nightmares with a child under three years.

- Sometimes it is possible to pin down nightmares to a certain activity. Your child may feel threatened by an aggressive child at playgroup, or have developed a fear of certain animals or people such as a policeman etc.

- A fear of the dark often contributes to a child having more frequent nightmares. Installing a low-voltage plug-in night light and buying a special new toy that will chase the monsters away often helps.

- Frequent late bedtimes, which usually result in a child getting over-tired and irritable, are often a cause, particularly when parents get short-tempered and cross. The child ends up going to bed exhausted, fretful and feeling unloved. He will then often wake in the night and remember how cross his parents were, then get upset and cry out. Although he will blame a bad dream, often the real cause for him crying out is a need for reassurance that his parents are no longer angry with him.

Case Study – Scarlett, aged 26 months

Problem: nightmares

Cause: video and story

Scarlett was two years and two months old when her parents first contacted me. She had always slept well at night and they always made sure that bedtime was a very calm and relaxing time.

But at around two years she had started to wake up one or two times a week, usually around 4.30am in the morning, screaming hysterically. She was insistent that there was a big woof-woof in the room. No matter how hard they tried, her parents could not convince her that there wasn't.

They would check under the bed and in all the cupboards but the more they tried to reassure her that there wasn't a woof-woof the more upset she would get. It could take well over an hour to settle her back to sleep and more often than not one of her parents would have to lie next to her on the bed. This pattern had been going on for six weeks, with the number of times Scarlett was waking in the night gradually increasing, when they contacted me.

I asked them if there had been any major changes in Scarlett's daily routine or bedtime routine, or the introduction of any new books or videos at bedtime. They assured me that nothing had changed over the last few months. They allowed Scarlett to watch 20 minutes of a video before her bath and then would read stories for 30 minutes or so after the bath.

I felt that Scarlett's imagination was probably developing

very quickly during this stage and that her very active mind was absorbing too many different thoughts prior to bed-time. Some of the stories and videos that had not had any effect on Scarlett in the past were possibly the cause of her nightmares, as she could now visualise a wolf eating Little Red Riding Hood or blowing down the little pigs' house.

I advised her parents to eliminate any videos or books that contained any form of violence in them and to reduce the amount of time she was allowed to watch the video. I also advised them to restrict storytelling after the bath to 15–20 minutes and choose stories that would fuel Scarlett's imag-ination with positive thoughts instead of fear. I suggested a change in bedtime routine which involved Scarlett beginning to learn to undress herself for the bath and put on her own nightclothes after the bath. This would help fill in the time that was previously spent watching videos and reading.

I advised the parents that it would be better not to get into a discussion in the middle of the night about whether or not there was a dog in the room, as Scarlett was too young to understand the difference between reality and dreaming. Instead they should pretend to chase the dog out of the room and reassure Scarlett that he couldn't get back in. Although Scarlett did continue to wake up crying and frightened of the imaginary dog, the wakings became less frequent and her parents were able to settle her back to sleep very quickly. Within a couple of weeks she was back to sleeping soundly right through the night.

I believe that books and videos play an important part of children's development, but between 18 months and three years of age the wrong types of books and videos can be a major cause of nightmares.

Night-terrors

Night-terrors are very different from nightmares and need to be dealt with differently. A child experiencing a night terror will usually wake up screaming during the earlier part of the night, usually within one to four hours of falling asleep. They occur during the non-REM sleep, often referred to as the deep sleep, and although a child having a night terror will scream, thrash around and have his eyes open, he is rarely awake. Whereas a child having a nightmare can be comforted, it can be very difficult to calm and comfort a child having a night-terror. It is very distressing for parents to watch a child having a night-terror as the child appears to be terrified, often sweating profusely and screaming as if he is experiencing something horrific. The majority of experts advise parents that unless the child shows signs of wanting to be held, it is better not to, as it often makes matters worse if the child becomes fully awake and is unaware of what has been happening. It is better to just stay close by so that if needed you can prevent him from injuring himself. A night-terror usually lasts between 10 and 20 minutes and provided the child is not woken up, he will settle back to sleep quickly once the terror is over. It is important not to mention the terror the following day, as your child may get very upset if questioned about something of which he has no recollection.

In my experience night-terrors are much more common amongst children who become over-tired because they have inconsistent day-time and bedtime routines. Dr Richard Ferber shares my view and says in his book that in very young children over-tiredness is the main cause of night-terrors. He advises that parents should ensure that their child gets sufficient sleep, and if necessary consider an earlier bedtime. He also emphasises the importance of a regular and consistent day-time routine.

Case Study – Daniel, aged 28 months

Problem: night terrors

Cause: over-tiredness

Daniel had always slept well, going through the night at 12 weeks, and apart from one occasion when he had had a cold he had never woken in the night. Therefore I was very surprised when his mother announced at 28 months that he had started to wake in the night. Having an extensive library of babycare books she could refer to, she very quickly realised that Daniel's waking was caused by night-terrors and not nightmares, as she had first imagined. He displayed all the typical behaviour of night-terrors that I have described above. His mother decided to follow the advice given by Penelope Leach in her book *Baby and Child*, putting on all the lights on in order to try and dispel the images she thought Daniel was seeing. She would use a soothing voice and the same familiar words to try to calm him, but would not attempt to wake him. Unfortunately, more often than not, Daniel would work himself up into an even worse state, yelling and screaming as he threw himself around the cot. When things reached this stage, she did as Leach advised and wiped Daniel's face with a warm, wet face cloth, which would wake him up.

Once awake, Daniel would have no recollection of the night-terror, but became so awake that it would then take his mother a further hour or so to settle him back to sleep. Daniel was a very happy, easy-going little boy, who ate a balanced diet and was emotionally stable. We discussed the problem many times but simply couldn't understand what was causing the terrors.

Many months later, on the first night of a five-day visit with the family, I observed Daniel's night-terrors first hand. I was convinced that turning on all the lights and trying to calm him down actually made matters worse, as he became even more agitated. I referred to Dr Richard Ferber's book for his view on the best way to deal with night terrors. His approach was the opposite to that of Penelope Leach. He advises parents against trying to calm the child and suggests that the child should only be held if he recognises them. The episode should be allowed to run its course and once the child shows signs of relaxing and calming down he can then be helped to lie back down and be tucked in. All this should be done without waking the child or talking to him.

Daniel's mother agreed to follow Ferber's advice the next time Daniel had a night-terror. She would enter the room without turning the light on, leaving the door slightly open so there was just enough light to see him. She would sit by his cot to ensure that he did not harm himself, but she wouldn't touch him or talk to him. The first night she did this Daniel sat up in his cot, eyes wide open, staring straight ahead, screaming and shouting incoherently for approximately six minutes, after which time he gave a big sigh and lay back down to sleep. The whole episode took approximately 10 minutes instead of the usual hour or more. From then on Daniel's mother used the Ferber method each time he had a night terror, which was usually once or twice a week.

With children under six years, over-tiredness is often the main cause of sleep terrors. I suggested to Daniel's parents that this might be the cause in his case. During my visit I had noticed that they had moved his bedtime from 7.30pm to nearer 9pm so that his mother could spend more time with him since her return to work. Because he was sleeping to 9am in the morning and still getting 12 hours sleep a night, his parents were not convinced that this was the case. However, they agreed to keep a diary of the times he went to bed and the nights he was woken by night-terrors.

They also agreed to try putting him to bed earlier on the days his mother didn't work. After a period of two weeks the notes showed that going to bed late for one night did not cause Daniel to have a night-terror but two late nights in a row did result in him having one. From then on they made sure that Daniel never had more than one late bed-time a week and he has never had a night-terror since.

Case Study – Callum, aged 36 months

Problem: getting out of bed

Cause: move to big bed

Callum was nearly three years old when I went to look after his new-born baby sister. He had always settled well around 8pm and slept through to 7.30/8am. However, when he was moved to a big bed a couple of months before the arrival of his sister, he immediately became more difficult to settle in the evening. Everything would go as normal until his parents turned off the light and left the room, but within minutes Callum would be out of his bed and appearing at the sitting-room door. He would get very upset when his parents took him back to his room, and it would take a further 10—15 minutes of talking to him and calming him down before they could leave the room. Over two weeks, the time he fell asleep had got progressively later until it was 9.30/10pm before he dropped off.

This performance would be repeated on and off all night. Some nights his parents were so exhausted that they wouldn't even attempt to settle Callum back in his bed when he came downstairs. By the time I arrived, it had reached a stage where Callum was only settling once his parents had gone upstairs to bed themselves. Once he knew that they were in their bedroom next door, he would calm down and settle to sleep, not getting out of bed until they went in and woke him at 7.30am. His parents had tried shutting the door and leaving him to cry, bribing him with presents and finally even getting angry and telling him off, but nothing seemed to break the pattern.

Because his night-time sleep had been reduced so dramatically, Callum had gone from being a happy little boy during the day to a very cranky one, and his behaviour at nursery had become very aggressive and disruptive. Once the new baby arrived, his mother, Lorna, became so exhausted trying to establish breastfeeding and deal with a very irritable child all afternoon that she reintroduced a short nap after lunch. While this improved Callum' s mood in the afternoon, it did not help with the settling in the evening. Because my booking was only for two weeks and her partner, James, was due to go away on a business trip for three weeks after I was due to leave, Lorna began to get very worried about how she was going to cope.

I explained to Lorna and James that this was not an unusual problem; many children who have always slept well will suddenly backtrack when they are transferred from a cot to a bed. Unlike other sleeping problems, this one is rarely helped by controlled crying. I suggested that the gradual withdrawal method would probably be the best approach and I agreed to help Lorna and James sort the problem out, provided that we remained consistent and persistent about taking Callum back to his room, no matter how many times it took. I felt that their inconsistency in the past had given him confusing signals. They had also allowed too much chatting while they were resettling him. He had to learn that this was quiet time and not time for talk and games.

I told Lorna and James that while they could reassure Callum if he was upset, they must use a very calm tone of voice and the same words at all times. I suggested that they say something like, 'It's quiet time now, Callum. Mummy and daddy are resting, and so must Callum.' It is very important with children of this age to keep repeating the same sentences over and over again, not allowing them to lead you into conversation about other things that may excite or upset them. I also suggested that we did not allow Callum the chance to get out of his bedroom and that Lorna or James should remain upstairs in their bedroom until we were sure Callum was asleep. This way they could stop him before he managed to get downstairs.

On the first night James did door-watch duty. He settled Callum in his bed at 7.3Opm, after his bedtime story, and explained to him that if he did not get out of bed he could have his little bedside light on and could read a book for a short time and that daddy would be back in a few minutes. He then left the room and stood outside, calling to Callum that he would be back in a few minutes and that he mustn't get out of bed. James only stayed out of the room for 30 seconds before going back in. He praised Callum for being such a good boy and quickly left the room again. This time he waited a minute before going back in, although he kept calling out to Callum, reminding him that he would be back in a few minutes and that he must be a good boy and stay in bed. James repeated this procedure, gradually increasing the length of time that he would stay out of the room, but continuing to remind Callum to stay in his bed and that daddy would come back in.

After about an hour, James had increased the time he was staying out of the room to ten minutes. That was when Callum made his first attempt to go downstairs. James managed to get to the door first and told him very firmly that if he did not get back in bed the door would be shut and the light turned off. Callum quickly got back into bed but within five minutes was again attempting to get downstairs. This time James carried out the threat and turned the light off and shut the door. Callum got very upset and screamed and shouted while trying to open the door. James held on to the handle so that Callum could not get out of the room and reassured him that if he got into bed and stayed there, he would open the door and turn the nightlight on. James opened the door for a few seconds every minute to repeat this reassurance. It took a further ten to fifteen minutes of protesting, but Callum finally got back into bed. James opened the door, switched on the nightlight and allowed Callum to choose another book to look at until he was ready to go to sleep. He then left the room again, calling out every minute or so to reassure Callum that he was just next door. He continued the checking procedure every ten minutes, and by 9.30pm Callum had fallen asleep. The next day we all gave Callum lots of praise for staying in his bed and gave him a star on his star chart. We explained that once he had three stars for staying in bed, we would take him on a special trip to the zoo.

The following three nights James followed the same procedure, gradually increasing the time he was out of the room but always reassuring Callum that daddy was just going to the loo or having a quick bath. By the fourth night, Callum had stopped attempting to get out of his room and James only needed to go in to him twice before he fell asleep somewhere between 8.30 and 9pm. Because Callum was not yet sleeping longer at night, I advised that his day-time nap should be eliminated so that he was tired at bedtime. By the ninth night Callum was happy to be left alone with his nightlight and a book and would normally fall asleep between 7.45 and 8pm. Although he had previously always slept in total darkness, I suggested that he be allowed to continue having the small beside light on until his parents went to bed, at which time they should plug in a glow-light and leave the door slightly ajar so that Callum did not wake up in the middle of the night to find himself in total darkness.

Case Study – Rory, aged 36 months

Problem: waking up wanting to play between 11pm and midnight

Cause: chocolate!

Jennifer first called me when Rory was two years and eleven months old. He was about to start at a nursery school that insisted that he should be out of nappies. Having attempted potty training twice and failed (each time it ended in tears and tantrums, with Rory refusing to go anywhere near the potty), Jennifer was determined that her third attempt would be a successful. She asked for my help in trying to find out why, despite Rory showing all the physical signs of bladder control and all the signs of mentally understanding the instructions he was given, previous attempts had ended in failure. After talking to Jennifer for about 10 minutes it became very obvious why potty training had not worked on either occasion.

While she thought she had followed to the letter all my advice in the book *Potty Training in One Week*, she had overlooked one very important point, that the child must be eager to participate in taking off his own clothes and be capable of helping to pull his own pants up and down.

Rory was still being totally dressed and undressed by his parents both times they attempted to potty train him, and I am sure that trying to learn two new skills at the same time left him feeling very frustrated and was the reason for him rebelling against potty training.

I advised her to put the potty away for at least two weeks and not even mention potty training. Instead she should concentrate on teaching him how to dress and undress himself. I suggested that she introduce a star chart with three different tasks on it. One of them should be a skill that he had already mastered so that he quickly understood that he got a star when he achieved a task.

Because Rory had a very stubborn streak I suggested that she explain that if he got four stars on his chart by the end of each day he could have two chocolate buttons after his tea in the evening. At the end of the first day Rory had worked so hard at achieving all his tasks that he had six stars on his chart. He was given the two chocolate buttons after his tea and, as always, settled easily to sleep at 7pm.

That same night, to the horror of his parents, Rory woke up at 11pm. He was not upset or confused, just bright as a button, wanting to chatter and play. It took his parents nearly an hour to settle him back to sleep. The same pattern happened for the next six nights. He would wake up happy and smiling and wanting to play for an hour or so before going back to sleep. His parents were totally baffled as, apart from when he had been ill, he had always slept soundly for 12 hours a night from the age of four months.

On the seventh night Jennifer's mother came to stay and over dinner they discussed all the possible reasons for Rory's late evening waking. Jennifer's mother was convinced that the cause of the problem was the two chocolate buttons that he had been given after his tea for the last seven nights. They decided that on the following night they would substitute a small fig biscuit for the chocolate buttons. Amazingly, Rory slept right through that night and has continued to do so ever since. His parents and grandmother are convinced that the chocolate was the cause of Rory's sudden night-time waking, and I agree with them. Apparently, Jennifer's elder brother had also been very sensitive to chocolate when he was a child, even the smallest amount would make him hyperactive.

At the beginning of the consultation I had asked Jennifer whether Rory reacted to chocolate. She had said that he didn't have it very often, but she couldn't recall him having any reactions. During the follow-up consultation it transpired that in the past he had never had chocolate late in the day.

I have always believed that certain foods can affect babies' and toddlers' sleep and since this consultation have kept a much closer eye not only on those foods that raise the blood sugar level, causing a temporary high, but also on the times at which the child is given these foods. There is indeed a link between the two and I now advise parents who are experiencing lively wakings in the night similar to Rory's to keep a detailed diary listing foods that boost the blood sugar levels.

The arrival of a new baby

The arrival of a new baby can often lead toddlers who have always slept well to start waking up in the night. This is very common and the best way to deal with it is to go straight to your toddler and reassure him that you are there. But try to keep the reassurance brief and not get involved in conversation or resort to taking him out of his bed. In my experience toddlers who are still sleeping in their cot seem have less waking in the night than those that have been transferred to a bed just prior to the birth of the baby.

Within a few weeks most toddlers settle down to sleeping well at night again. If this doesn't happen, it is advisable to look for other reasons why your child is waking. Establishing regular day-time naps where your baby is put to sleep away from the toddler means that you can give your toddler your undivided attention at regular times during the day. This will help him feel more secure than a toddler who is suddenly faced with having to share his mother every waking hour of the day. If he doesn't seem overly interested in the baby, try not to force the issue. He will start to take an interest in his own time; pressurising him to do so before he is ready will only make him feel more resentful towards the baby.

In the very early days try to structure as many of the baby's feeds as possible for when your toddler is not around, for example before he gets up in the morning and around 2pm while he is having his nap. Of course there will be times when he will be around when the baby is feeding, but until he gets used to sharing you with the baby, the less he sees the baby on your breast the better.

The big bed

In my experience, transferring a toddler to a big bed before he is ready can be a major cause of night-time waking. Many parents make this transfer between 18 months and two years of age, often prompted by the fact a new baby is on the way and the cot will be needed. Other parents listen to the advice of friends who say that their todder sleeps much better now he is in a bed. To me this implies that their toddler's sleeping habits were probably not very good in the first place!

The majority of my clients leave their toddlers in a cot until they are nearly three years of age. Because all of these toddlers are still sleeping in a sleeping bag, the possibility of them trying to climb out of the cot never arises. If a cot is needed for a second baby, many parents choose to buy a second cot, or a cot bed into which the toddler can be transferred before the new baby arrives. This can eventually be used as a first bed for the second baby.

Before transferring your toddler to a bed consider the following points.

- A toddler who is transferred to a bed too early is more likely to wake up early or get up in the night. He is inclined to get more upset than an older child when parents try to settle him back to sleep in his own bed, and often ends up sleeping in his parents' bed.

- The arrival of a new baby often prompts the toddler to get out of bed if he hears the baby crying in the night. He quickly learns to demand the same attention as the baby in the night – feeds and a cuddle.

- A toddler who is potty-trained and sleeping in a bed will be more likely to take his nappy off in the night, even if he is not able to get through the night without a nappy.

- Once the nappy is abandoned at night, a potty and night light usually have to be put in the toddler's room. In my experience, toddlers under three years of age who are sleeping in a bed and who need to have a night light are much more likely to wake in the night and be difficult to settle back to sleep.

Useful addresses

Baby equipment
The Great Little Trading Company
124 Walcot Street
Bath BA1 5BG
Tel: 0870 241 4082

Black out lining & roller blinds
Available from all John Lewis Partnership stores throughout the UK.

Cotton sleeping bags
Kiddycare (Mail order)
Tel: 01309 674646
Fax: 01309 674646

Organisations
The Foundation for the Study of Infant Deaths
Artillery House
11–19 Artillery Row
London SW1P 1RT
Helpline: 0870 787 0554
Tel: 0870 787 0885
Fax: 0870 787 0725
Email: fsid@sids.org.uk

For a personal telephone consultation with Gina Ford or details of her parenting classes, workshops and seminars in your area telephone: 01298 303351.

Or you can find her on her new website: www.contendedbaby.com

Further reading

From Contented Baby to Confident Child by Gina Ford (Vermilion, 2000)

The New Contented Little Baby Book by Gina Ford (Vermilion, 2002)

The Great Ormond Street New Baby and Child Care Book (Vermilion, 1997)

New Toddler Taming by Dr Christopher Green (Vermilion, 2001)

Three in a Bed by Deborah Jackson (Bloomsbury, 2003)

Your Baby & Child by Penelope Leach (Dorling Kindersley, 2003)

The New Baby and Toddler Sleep Programme by Professor John Pearce with Jane Bidder (Vermilion, 1999)

Your New Baby by Dr Miriam Stoppard (Dorling Kindersley, 1998)

Index

By Gina Ford
Also available from Vermilion